CD-ROM INCLUDED

Repro

• More than 150 coloring pages
• Balance of Old and New Testament stories
• Bible story printed on back of each page
• 34 bonus pages on CD-ROM

COLORING PAGES
BIBLE STORY
BIG BOOK
OF
REALLY

Gospel Light's

MW00789473

Guidelines for Photocopying/Reproducing Pages

Permission to make photocopies of or to reproduce by any other mechanical or electronic means in whole or in part any designated* page, illustration or activity in this book is granted only to the original purchaser and is intended for noncommercial use within a church or other Christian organization. None of the material in this book may be reproduced for any commercial promotion, advertising or sale of a product or service. Sharing of the material in this book with other churches or organizations not owned or controlled by the original purchaser is also prohibited. All rights reserved.

*Pages with the following notation can be legally reproduced:

© 2007 Gospel Light. Permission to photocopy granted to original purchaser only. *The Really Big Book of Bible Story Coloring Pages*

Editorial Staff

Founder, Dr. Henrietta Mears • **Publisher,** William T. Greig • **Senior Consulting Publisher,** Dr. Elmer L. Towns
• **Senior Managing Editor,** Sheryl Haystead • **Senior Consulting Editor,** Wesley Haystead, M.S.Ed.
• **Senior Editor, Biblical and Theological Issues,** Bayard Taylor, M.Div. • **Associate Editor,** Veronica Neal
• **Art Director,** Samantha A. Hsu • **Designer,** Lenndy Pollard

Scripture quotations are taken from the *Holy Bible, New International Version®.*
Copyright © 1973, 1978, 1984 by International Bible Society.
Used by permission of Zondervan Publishing House. All rights reserved.

These coloring pages originally published in *Bible Story Coloring Pages* (Ventura, CA: Gospel Light, 1997)
and *Bible Story Coloring Pages #2* (Ventura, CA: Gospel Light, 2002).

This book is not affiliated with or licensed by Really Big Coloring Books, Inc.

Great Ways to Use These Pages:

❀ **Storytelling Tool:** Photocopy the Bible story coloring page to use as a visual aid during storytelling time. As you tell the story, color in parts of the picture to keep children's interest and to help them focus on the part of the story you are telling. For larger groups, make transparencies and color them on an overhead projector as you tell the story.

❀ **Felt Board Figures:** Glue a colored Bible story coloring page to poster board. Cut out the main characters and then glue strips of felt to the backs of the characters. Use them with a felt board to give visual impact to your Bible storytelling.

❀ **Story Review:** Photocopy a coloring page for each student. After telling the story, ask questions to review the story as children color.

❀ **Review for Early Arrivals and Transition Times:** Photocopy coloring pages of Bible stories you have recently talked about. Early arrivals can have a choice of pictures to color, giving you opportunities to ask questions and talk with children about those stories. Also have copies available for children who finish an activity ahead of others and for other transition times.

❀ **Coloring Game:** After you've told the Bible story, place a variety of colored markers on the table. Distribute copies of the Bible story coloring page. Volunteers tell one part of the Bible story. Then each child chooses a marker and uses it to color one part of his or her page. When they're finished, children put markers down and volunteers tell another part of the story. Children then choose another marker and color another part of the page. Repeat the process until the pages (and story!) are completed.

✺ **Concentration Game:** Photocopy a set of two pictures of each story you have talked about recently. Invite volunteers to color each set alike. Then place the pictures facedown on the floor. Children take turns turning over two pictures at a time, trying to find two matching pictures. Play continues until all picture sets have been paired.

✺ **Guessing Game:** Color (or invite volunteers to color) five or more coloring pages of Bible stories you have talked about. Display completed pictures. Give three clues for a story. Children try to guess which story you are describing. For example, for "Jesus is born" you could say, "I'm thinking of a happy night. I'm thinking of some good news that some people heard. I'm thinking of a very special baby."

✺ **Individual Coloring Books:** Photocopy several Bible story coloring pages for each child in your class. Fold 11x17-inch (28x43-cm) construction paper in half, insert pages and staple to make individual coloring books.

✺ **Bible Story Puzzle:** Color and then paste a completed Bible story coloring page onto poster board. Cover with clear adhesive paper and cut into puzzle pieces. Place puzzle pieces in a resealable sandwich bag and label. Make several puzzles and offer them during transition times or to early arrivals.

✺ **Puppets:** Color (or invite children to color) the main characters on the Bible story coloring page. Glue the colored page to poster board. Cut around the figures and glue the characters to craft sticks. Give to children to use as stick puppets.

✺ **Parent Involvement:** Send home with children two copies of a Bible story coloring page with the story photocopied on the back. Include a note to encourage parents to read the Bible story and color the pages with their children.

✺ **Special Gift:** Give this book to your children as a great substitute for secular coloring books.

Table of Contents

Old Testament

New Testament

Bonus CD-ROM Bible Stories

Old Testament

New Testament

Matthew 2:1-12 • Wise men travel to find Jesus

Luke 2:21-38 • Simeon and Anna welcome Jesus

John 4:43-54 • Jesus helps a young boy become well

John 5:1-15 • Jesus makes a sick man well

Matthew 9:18-26; Mark 5:22-43; Luke 8:40-56 • Jesus heals Jairus's daughter

Matthew 16:13-20 • Peter says Jesus is God's Son

Luke 12:13-21 • Jesus talks about a rich man

Luke 15:8-10 • A woman finds a special coin

Luke 18:9-14 • Two men pray

Luke 10:38-42 • Mary listens to Jesus

Mark 10:46-52; Luke 18:35-43 • Jesus heals blind Bartimaeus

Acts 4:32-37 • Barnabas shows his love for Jesus by sharing

Acts 14:8-18 • Paul and Barnabas visit Lystra

Acts 28 • Paul teaches about Jesus

Philemon 1-25 • Paul sends Onesimus home

God creates the world.

Genesis 1:1—2:25

God creates the world.

Genesis 1:1—2:25

In the beginning, before anything was anything, God made the heavens and the earth. He just said, "Let there be light," and there was light! Then God made the sky and the land and the oceans. God made the plants and the sun, moon and stars. He liked what He made. It was very good!

Then God said, "Let the sky be filled with birds that fly." And it was. He said, "Let the waters be filled with all sorts of creatures." Then there were fish, dolphins, jellyfish, and many other creatures in the water. Next, God made every kind of animal. When God saw all the creatures that He made, He said that they were very good.

Then God did something even more special! He took some dirt and formed it into a man. Then God breathed into the man and he became alive. Next, God made a woman. They were the first people—people like you and me. They were named Adam and Eve. God loved Adam and Eve. Everything God made was very good.

Adam and Eve disobey God.
Genesis 3:1-24

Adam and Eve disobey God.

Genesis 3:1-24

Adam and Eve lived in a wonderful garden. There were trees and plants with good food like apples, bananas, grapes and watermelon. There were flowers and trees and plants that were beautiful to look at.

In the middle of the garden was a tree called the tree of the knowledge of good and evil. God told Adam and Eve they could eat anything in the whole garden except the fruit that was growing on that one tree.

One day, a serpent talked to Eve and told her to eat the forbidden fruit. "If you eat some of that fruit, you would know things you didn't know before," the snake said. "You would be like God."

Eve listened to the serpent. She ate some of the fruit from the tree that God said not to eat from. Adam ate some, too. God was very sad that they had disobeyed Him. Adam and Eve had to leave the beautiful garden, but God still loved them very much.

Cain and Abel give offerings.
Genesis 4:1-16

Cain and Abel give offerings.

Genesis 4:1-16

Adam and Eve had two sons. Their names were Cain and Abel. The boys learned how to do different kinds of jobs to help their family. Cain, the older brother, was a farmer. Abel, the younger brother, grew up to be a shepherd.

Soon it was time to thank God for everything He had given to Adam and Eve's family. Cain brought an offering of some vegetables he had grown. Abel brought some of his sheep.

Abel had given thanks to God by giving Him the best gift he could. God was happy with the offering Abel brought. But God was not pleased with Cain's offering. This made Cain angry. God told Cain to do what was right. Then his offering would please God. God said that if Cain didn't do what was right, more trouble would come. Cain didn't listen to God's warning and more trouble came. One day, when Cain and Abel were out in a field, Cain killed Abel.

God called to Cain, "Where is your brother, Abel?" Cain was angry and said to God, "I don't know where he is. Do I have to take care of my brother all the time?"

God knew Cain had killed Abel. God told Cain he would have to leave his home and stop being a farmer. Cain's trouble came because he did not love and obey God.

Noah builds the ark.
Genesis 6

Noah builds the ark.

Genesis 6

After God made the world, more and more people were born. But as the years went by, people forgot about God. They said things that were not true. They took things that did not belong to them. They did things to hurt each other. They didn't obey God.

But there was a man named Noah. Noah loved God. He did what was right. One day God said, "Noah, I am going to stop all the terrible things that people keep doing. I want you to build a big wooden boat." This big boat was called an ark.

God told Noah that He was going to send a lot of rain. The rain would make a big flood. The whole earth would be covered with water! But Noah and his family would be safe inside the big boat.

God told him how tall and how long to make the boat. God told Noah what kind of wood to use. God even told Noah where to put the window and the door!

Noah and his family obeyed God. They started building the big boat. Noah and his three sons cut down trees. They sawed the wood into boards. They hammered the boards together. Noah and his family worked hard to make the boat just the way God had said.

Finally the boat was finished! Noah and his family were ready for the flood of water. They were glad God told them to build the big boat. They knew God was taking care of them.

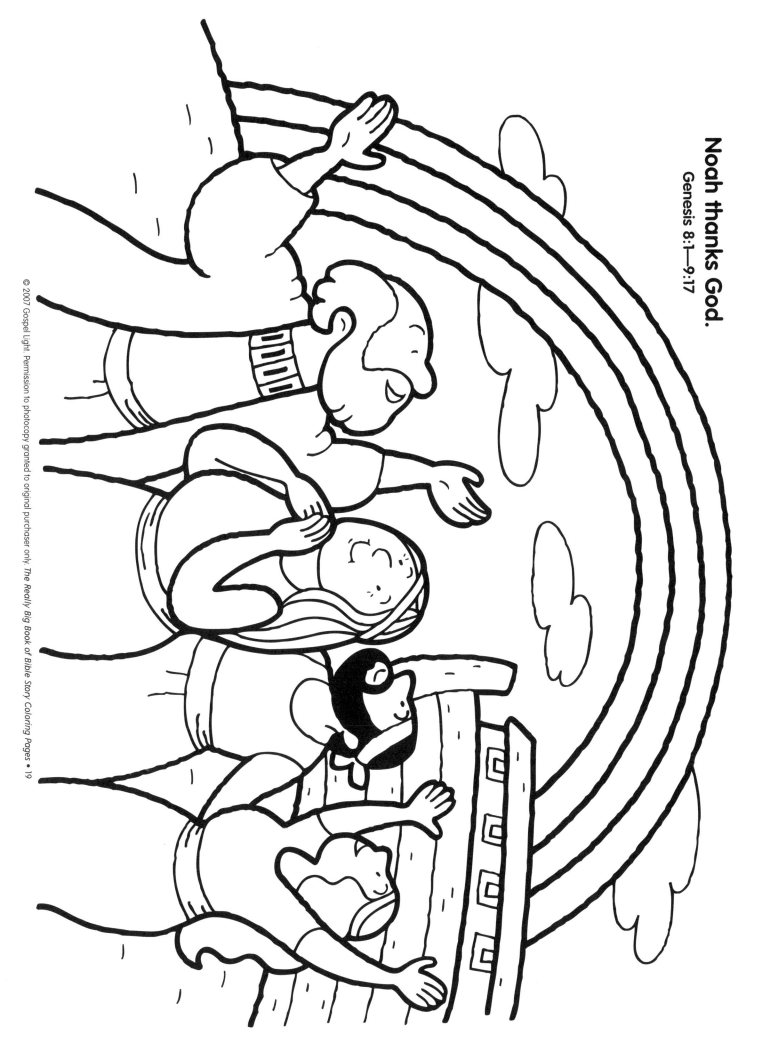

Noah thanks God.
Genesis 8:1—9:17

Noah thanks God.

Genesis 8:1—9:17

It had rained for 40 days and 40 nights. There was water everywhere! But finally, it stopped raining. God made a wind blow over the earth to dry up the water from the flood. It took days and days and weeks and weeks for the water to dry up. Noah and his family were shut up inside the big boat for a long time!

But one day God said, "Noah, come out of the ark now. Bring your family with you. And bring all those birds and other animals that have been living in the ark with you, too."

What an exciting day that must have been! Noah and his family and all the animals paraded out of the big boat. When Noah got outside, the first thing he and his family did was to thank God for keeping him and his family safe during the flood.

God made a special promise to Noah. God promised, "I will NEVER again cover the whole earth with a flood." To remind everyone of His promise, God put a beautiful rainbow in the sky. Of course, Noah and his family remembered God's promise every time they saw a rainbow! And even now, whenever we see a rainbow, we can remember that God always keeps His promises. We can remember that God loves us and will always take care of us.

God stops the building of a tower.

Genesis 11:1-9

God stops the building of a tower.

Genesis 11:1-9

After Noah and his family left the ark, Noah's family grew. Soon there were many, many people. And every family had many, many sheep and goats! The people moved from place to place to find enough clean water and fresh grass for their animals.

One day the people found a wonderful place to live between two rivers. Grass, fruit trees and vegetables grew well there. The people built houses there. They learned to build strong buildings out of baked bricks and tar. They planned to build a city. The city would have a tall tower. Their tower would show everyone how strong and smart they were. They were so proud of themselves!

But they did not ask for God's help! They only thought of themselves. So God decided it was time to stop the people from being so proud of themselves. God made all the people speak different languages!

Suddenly the men who were building the tall tower could not understand each other. They did not know whether someone asked them for bricks or for hay. Because they could not understand each other, they had to stop building the tower! God showed that He was stronger and smarter than these proud people.

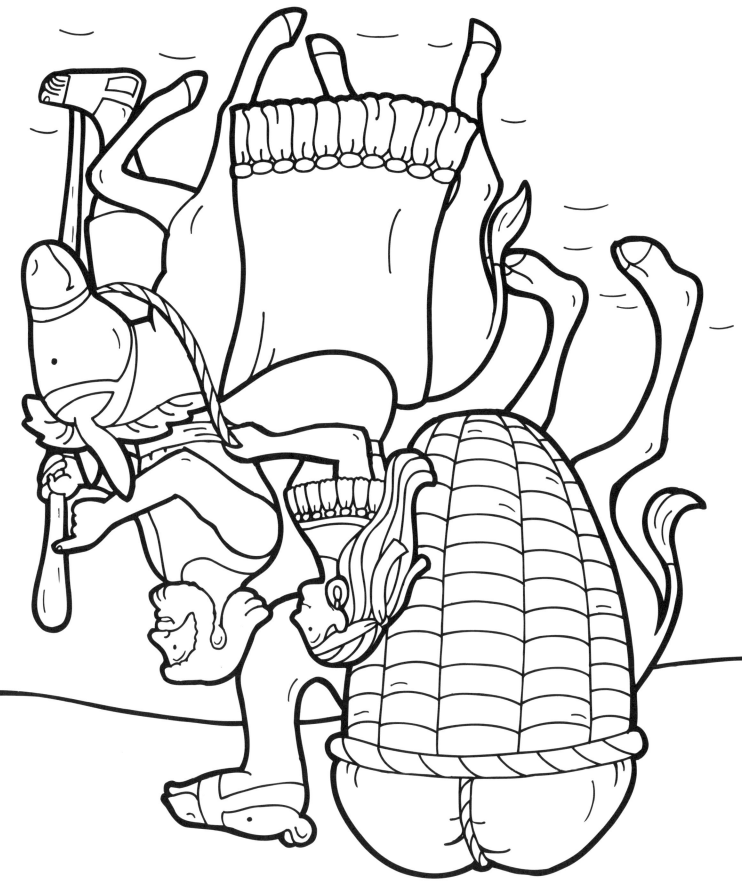

Abram travels to a new home.
Genesis 12:1-9

Abram travels to a new home.

Genesis 12:1-9

God loved Abram. God told Abram to leave his home and go to a new land. God promised to make Abram the leader of a great nation.

Abram obeyed God. He and his wife and his nephew, Lot, left their home. They took all their animals and their helpers with them. They walked for many, many days.

After days and days of walking, Abram and his family arrived in the new land. God told him that He was going to give the land to Abram's children. Abram worshiped God. Abram trusted God. Abram believed that God would keep His promises.

Isaac is born.
Genesis 15:1-6; 17:1-8; 18:1-15; 21:1-7

Isaac is born.

Genesis 15:1-6; 17:1-8; 18:1-15; 21:1-7

God gave a special promise to Abram. He promised to give Abram and his wife a son. As a reminder of His promise, God changed Abram's name to Abraham. Abraham means "father of many." Abraham and his wife, Sarah, waited many years but they still did not have a child. Abraham still did not stop believing God's promise.

Abraham and Sarah grew very old, older than most grandparents. One day some angels visited Abraham. "Next year Sarah will have a son," the visitors said.

Sarah was sitting in her tent listening to Abraham and the visitors. When she heard the angels' words, she started to laugh. She and Abraham were almost one hundred years old! She knew that no one her age ever had a baby. She was just too old! The visitors knew that she laughed. They said, "Is anything too hard for God?"

God kept His promise to Abraham and Sarah. The next year, Sarah had a baby boy just as God had said. Abraham and Sarah named him Isaac.

Abraham obeys God.
Genesis 22:1-19

Abraham obeys God.

Genesis 22:1-19

Abraham and Sarah were happy. They had a baby boy named Isaac. God had promised that they would have many grandchildren and great-grandchildren from Isaac. All these people would help others learn about God's love.

God wanted to make sure that Abraham would always obey God's instructions and follow Him.

God told Abraham to take his son Isaac and offer him to God, like he would offer a goat or a lamb on an altar. But this meant Isaac would die! Abraham was very sad. Abraham must have wondered why God wanted him to do this. But Abraham decided to obey God.

Abraham and Isaac walked up to the top of a nearby mountain. When they got to the top,

Abraham built an altar. Isaac asked Abraham where the animal was for the offering. Abraham told Isaac that God would provide the animal. Then Abraham tied Isaac's feet and hands and set him on top of the altar.

At that moment, Abraham heard a voice. It was an angel sent by God. The angel told Abraham to STOP. God knew that Abraham had obeyed him.

Abraham heard a noise. He saw an animal called a ram. The ram was stuck in the bushes. God had provided the animal for the offering! Abraham thanked God! Abraham quickly untied Isaac and offered the ram to God. Abraham must have been glad he had obeyed God. And God knew that Abraham would always obey Him.

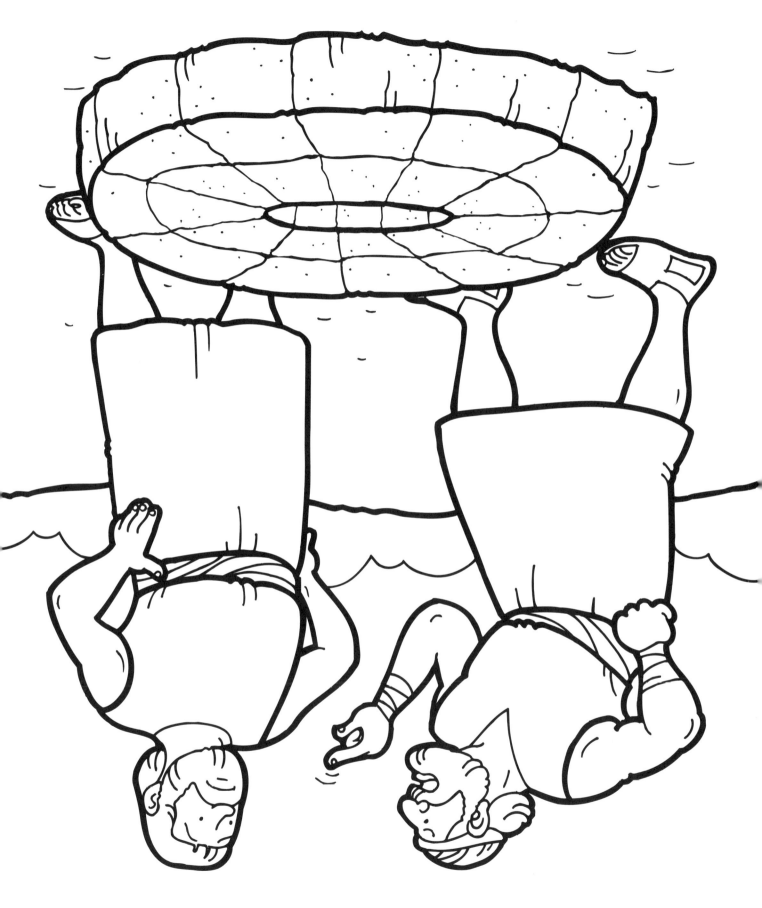

Isaac chooses not to fight.
Genesis 26:12-33

Isaac chooses not to fight.

Genesis 26:12-33

Isaac needed to dig a well so his family and his helpers and his animals could have good water to drink. Isaac's helpers worked hard digging deep into the ground. Then, water began to fill up the hole!

Everyone was happy except Isaac's neighbors. They shouted, "That well is ours!" Isaac did not want to fight with his neighbors. So Isaac let them have the well. Isaac moved on to another place. He told his helpers to dig another well.

The helpers worked hard again. Soon water began to fill up the hole. But then Isaac's neighbors came again. "That well is ours!" they shouted.

Isaac still wanted to be kind to his neighbors. So Isaac moved to another place again. And he told his helpers to dig another well. That night God said to Isaac, "Do not be afraid, Isaac. I will always be with you."

Isaac's neighbors came again. They said, "We will not fight with you any more." Isaac was very happy! Isaac was glad God had helped him to be kind.

Jacob tricks Isaac.

Genesis 27:1-45

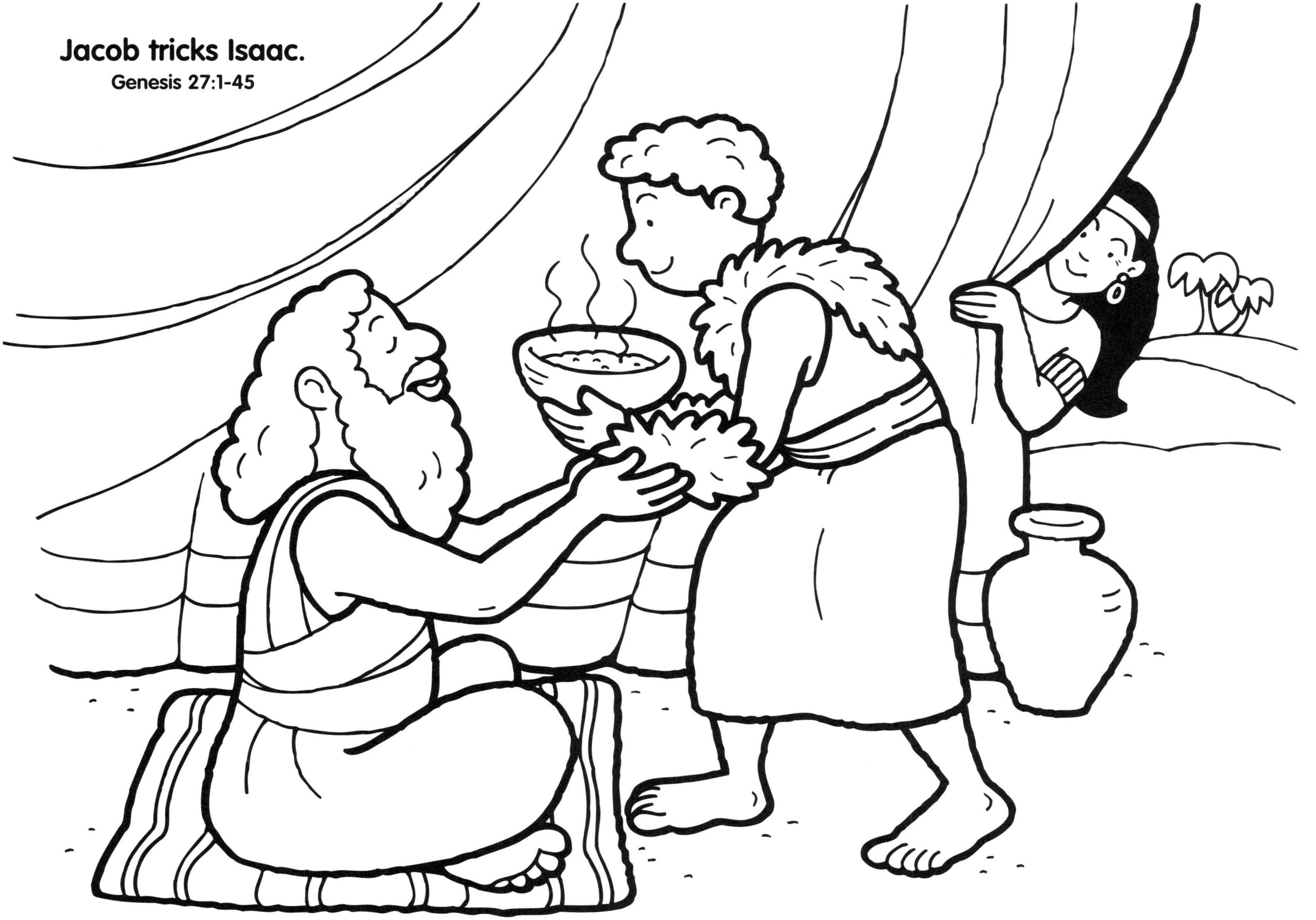

Jacob tricks Isaac.

Genesis 27:1-45

Isaac had two grown-up sons named Jacob and Esau. One day Isaac told Esau, "I am getting old. I want to give you my blessing before I die." (The blessing was a special promise given to the family's new leader.) Isaac wanted Esau to be that new leader. Isaac asked Esau to go hunting and cook Isaac's favorite food. Then Isaac would give Esau the blessing. Esau went hunting right away!

But Jacob and Esau's mother, Rebekah, wanted Jacob to be the new leader of the family, instead of Esau. She told Jacob, "We will get the blessing for you instead. Quickly, while Esau is gone, do what I tell you."

Rebekah told Jacob to put on Esau's clothes. This made Jacob smell like Esau. She put hairy pieces of goatskin on Jacob's hands and neck. This made Jacob feel more like Esau, because Esau had a lot of hair. Isaac could not see very well, so

Rebekah and Jacob hoped Isaac would think Jacob WAS Esau! Rebekah made Isaac's favorite meal.

Jacob took the food to his father. Then he told a lie. "It's me, Esau," Jacob said. "I've made your favorite food." The tricks worked! Isaac said, "It sounds like Jacob's voice, but these hands feel like Esau's."

After Isaac ate, he asked God to give his son many good things. He asked God to make his son a great leader. Isaac's prayer was called a blessing. He thought he was blessing Esau. But he was really blessing Jacob!

Soon Esau came home. When Esau found out Jacob had tricked their father, he was very angry. He wanted to hurt Jacob! Jacob had to go away for many years. Because Jacob didn't do what was right, his family was sad and angry.

Jacob goes home.
Genesis 31:1—33:20

Jacob goes home.

Genesis 31:1—33:20

Jacob lived with his uncle for a long time. Jacob had many sheep, goats, donkeys and camels. Jacob got married and had many children. After many years, God told Jacob it was time to go back home to the land where he used to live.

Jacob took his wives and children and all his animals and servants. They left Jacob's uncle's farm and traveled to the place God told them to go. But Jacob was afraid to go home.

Jacob was afraid because when he was younger, he had cheated his brother, Esau. Esau had been very angry and had wanted to hurt Jacob. Jacob was afraid that Esau would still want to hurt him. Jacob was afraid that Esau might still be so angry that he would hurt Jacob's family. So Jacob asked God to help him. And God took care of Jacob. Esau forgave Jacob and was kind to him.

Esau forgives Jacob.
Genesis 32:3-21; 33:1-11

Esau forgives Jacob.

Genesis 32:3-21; 33:1-11

Jacob and Esau were brothers. Jacob had tricked their father, Isaac, and took important things that were Esau's. Esau was angry with Jacob, so Jacob ran far away! He stayed for many years, got married and had many children in that faraway place.

One day God told Jacob to go back home. Jacob and his family packed their belongings and started out on the long trip. Jacob was worried that Esau was still angry. So Jacob sent some of his helpers to tell Esau he was coming home. The helpers came back and told Jacob, "Esau is coming to meet you. He has 400 men with him!"

Jacob was afraid. Four hundred men sounded like an army! Jacob prayed. He asked God to keep him and his family safe. Then Jacob sent Esau a gift of many animals. Jacob and his family walked far behind the animals. Finally, they could see Esau and his 400 men coming.

As Jacob walked toward Esau, Jacob bowed low, over and over again. Jacob was sorry for the wrong things he had done. Esau began to run toward Jacob. Esau came up to Jacob and hugged him! Esau forgave Jacob! The two brothers cried and hugged each other some more. They were friends again.

Joseph's brothers sell him.

Genesis 37:2-36

Joseph's brothers sell him.

Genesis 37:2-36

Joseph's father, Jacob, loved Joseph more than any of Joseph's other brothers. Jacob gave Joseph a special coat to show that Joseph was his favorite son. Joseph had dreams about being in charge of the family even though he was one of the youngest brothers. Joseph's brothers thought that Joseph was always bragging.

One day Jacob sent Joseph to check on his brothers while they were taking care of the sheep. Joseph walked a long time. Finally he found his brothers and the sheep.

When his brothers saw Joseph coming, they decided to get rid of Joseph by throwing him into a dry well. While the brothers were eating lunch, they saw a caravan headed for Egypt. They pulled Joseph out of the well and sold him as a slave to the people in the caravan.

Then Joseph's brothers took Joseph's coat and tore it up so that it looked like a wild animal had attacked him. They told their father, Jacob, that they found Joseph's coat in a field. Jacob was sad because he thought that Joseph was dead.

Joseph helps Pharaoh.
Genesis 39:1—41:49

Joseph helps Pharaoh.

Genesis 39:1—41:49

Joseph was sold as a slave to an Egyptian official. Later, Joseph was put in prison because the official's wife told a lie about him. But God took care of Joseph. God helped Joseph talk to Pharaoh (the king)!

Joseph warned Pharaoh that there would be seven years when lots of food would grow in the fields and then seven years when no food would grow in the fields. "You need to put someone in charge of collecting food. Then when there is no food growing in the fields, there will still be food for everyone to eat."

Pharaoh liked what Joseph said. He put Joseph in charge of collecting food. Pharaoh gave Joseph a ring and some fancy new clothes. He even gave Joseph a chariot to ride in!

Joseph traveled all over Egypt and made sure that there would be plenty of food to eat for everyone. God helped Joseph take care of all the people.

Joseph forgives his brothers.

Genesis 42:1—45:28

Joseph forgives his brothers.

Genesis 42:1—45:28

Jacob's family didn't have any food. Jacob heard that there was food to buy in Egypt. He sent Joseph's brothers there to buy food. Joseph's brothers didn't know that God had helped Joseph become an important ruler in Egypt.

When Joseph's brothers got to Egypt, they asked to buy food. They did not know they were talking to Joseph. It had been a long time since they had seen Joseph. Joseph had grown up. Now he dressed and talked like an Egyptian.

Joseph pretended that he did not know his brothers. He asked them about their family. Joseph tested them to see if they were sorry for being mean to him. Then Joseph told his brothers who he was, and he forgave them. Joseph invited them all to come and live near him in Egypt. Joseph was glad to be with his family again.

The people of Israel are slaves in Egypt.

Exodus 1:1-22

The people of Israel are slaves in Egypt.

Exodus 1:1-22

Joseph's brothers and father and all their families moved to Egypt. They lived there for many years. They had children and their children had children. They were called Israelites. Soon there were many Israelites in Egypt.

There was a new king in Egypt now. This Pharaoh didn't know the good things that Joseph had done for his country. He was afraid of the Israelites because there were so many of them. He thought they might take over the country. The new Pharaoh made the Israelites his slaves. That means he made them work hard and didn't pay them.

Even though the Egyptians treated the Israelite slaves very badly, God had a plan to help the Israelites.

God protects baby Moses.

Exodus 2:1-10

God protects baby Moses.

Exodus 2:1-10

Pharaoh was afraid of the Israelites. There were many Israelites in Egypt. Pharaoh thought there were too many Israelites. Pharaoh planned to stop them by hurting all the Israelite baby boys.

But one mother hid her baby boy from the Egyptian soldiers. When she couldn't hide him anymore, she made a basket that would float. She put the baby in the basket and carefully put it on the river. The baby's big sister, Miriam, hid nearby to watch what would happen.

Pharaoh's daughter came to the river with her servants to take a bath. The princess saw the basket and sent one of her servants to get it. When she opened the basket, the baby was crying. The Princess felt sorry for him.

Miriam ran up to the princess and said, "Shall I go and get someone to take care of this baby for you?" The princess said yes. So Miriam brought her mother to the princess. The princess told the mother to take care of the baby. Later the princess named the baby Moses. When Moses grew up, he lived with the princess, right in the Pharaoh's palace!

God talks to Moses.
Exodus 3:1—4:17

God talks to Moses.

Exodus 3:1—4:17

Grown-up Moses went to live in the desert. He took care of some sheep. One day he saw something strange. A bush was on fire, but it did not burn up! Moses walked near the bush to see why it didn't burn up.

God spoke to Moses from the bush. He said, "Moses, take off your shoes. This is a holy place." Moses knew it was God talking. God said, "Moses, tell Pharaoh to let my people go free." God did not want the Israelites to be slaves anymore. God wanted Moses to be the leader of the Israelites.

Moses was afraid. He was afraid that Pharaoh would not listen to him. Moses was afraid that the Israelites would not listen to him.

God told Moses that He would help Moses do what God wanted. Moses would even be able to do miracles. Then Pharaoh would do what God wanted. But Moses was still afraid. So God told Moses that Moses' brother Aaron would help him. Finally, Moses was ready to go talk to Pharaoh.

Moses says,
"Let my people go."
Exodus 5:1—12:32

Moses says, "Let my people go."

Exodus 5:1—12:32

Moses went to Pharaoh. "God said to let His people go," Moses said. Pharaoh did not listen. Pharaoh did not care about what God said. Instead, he made the Israelites work even harder!

Moses went to see Pharaoh again. He told Pharaoh, "God is going to send terrible troubles on Egypt if you do not let the Israelites go." Pharaoh didn't care. He said no again!

God made terrible things happen in Egypt because Pharaoh would not listen to God. The troubles got worse and worse. Frogs came out of the river and got into everything. There were bugs everywhere. All the animals in the fields died. People got terrible sores and all the plants were destroyed. But Pharaoh still refused to let the Israelites go.

Finally, even Pharaoh's own son died. Then Pharaoh knew that God was powerful. Pharaoh told Moses and the Israelites to leave.

Moses leads the people out of Egypt.
Exodus 12:33-39; 13:17-22

Moses leads the people out of Egypt.

Exodus 12:33-39; 13:17-22

God wanted His people to leave Egypt and go on a long trip to a new home. The people packed everything they had. They gathered all their animals. There were hundreds of thousands of people! That's more than you would want to count!

Moses told the people, "God will take care of us. God will lead us and show us the way."

During the day, God put a big, white cloud in the sky. The people followed the cloud. During the night, God put fire in the sky. The people followed the fire.

All of the people and animals walked behind God's cloud during the day and behind God's fire during the night. The people were glad they were going to a new home. They were glad God showed them He was with them. The people knew God was taking care of them on their long trip.

God makes a path through the Red Sea. Exodus 14:1-31

God makes a path through the Red Sea.
Exodus 14:1-31

Pharaoh wanted the Israelites to come back to Egypt. He didn't have enough slaves left to do all the work the Israelites had done before they left.

So Pharaoh and his army chased after the Israelites. When the people saw the army coming, they were afraid. They couldn't run away because they were at the edge of the Red Sea.

But God took care of His people. God told Moses to hold his hand out over the Red Sea. God sent a strong wind that blew and blew and made a path of dry land through the Red Sea. The people walked through the sea on dry ground!

The Egyptian army tried to follow them. When all the Israelites were safe on the other side, God told Moses to stretch his hand out over the sea again. The water went back into its place. Whoosh! The Egyptian army was covered up by the water.

All the Israelites trusted God because of the way He saved them from the Egyptians.

God gives water to the Israelites.

Exodus 15:22-27

God gives water to the Israelites.

Exodus 15:22-27

God was leading the Israelites and their animals on a long trip, away from Egypt. They walked through the hot desert. There were not many trees for shade. There was not much water to drink. There was just a lot of hot sand.

"We're hot," God's people said. "We're thirsty!" The sun got hotter and hotter. Their water was just about all gone.

Then someone shouted, "Look! Water!" The people hurried to the edge of the water. They took big drinks—but then they stopped. "This water tastes bad!" the people complained. "Moses, what are we going to do?"

Moses knew God loved His people. Moses asked God what to do. God showed Moses a special piece of wood. He told Moses to throw the wood into the water. Moses did what God said.

After Moses threw in the wood, someone leaned over and took a sip of water. And then another person did. "It tastes good!" the people shouted. Everyone drank and drank! They splashed their faces and filled their water bags. God had given them water when they needed it. They were glad!

God gives manna to eat.

Exodus 16:1-36

God gives manna to eat.

Exodus 16:1-36

The people were hungry. They had been traveling in the desert for many days. They didn't have any more good food to eat. The people started to complain. They forgot that God would take care of them.

God told Moses that He was going to give His people food from heaven.

The next morning there were strange white flakes all around on the ground. "This is bread from the Lord," Moses told the people. The people called the bread manna. It tasted like crackers made with honey. All the people worked together to pick up the manna. Every day each person had enough to eat.

God gives the Ten Commandments.

Exodus 19:1—24:18

God gives the Ten Commandments.

Exodus 19:1—24:18

The Israelites walked in the desert for many days. They came to a mountain. God told them to camp by the mountain. All the people set up tents. They gathered fuel and made fires to cook food on. They found places for their animals to rest and eat.

God told Moses to come up to the top of the mountain. God wanted to talk with Moses. God told Moses many things while Moses was on the mountain. God gave Moses two stone tablets that God wrote His laws on. God told Moses many more laws for the people to follow. God's laws helped the people know what God wanted. God's laws told the people to be fair to each other.

Moses went down from the mountain and told the Israelites everything God had told him. The people promised to obey God.

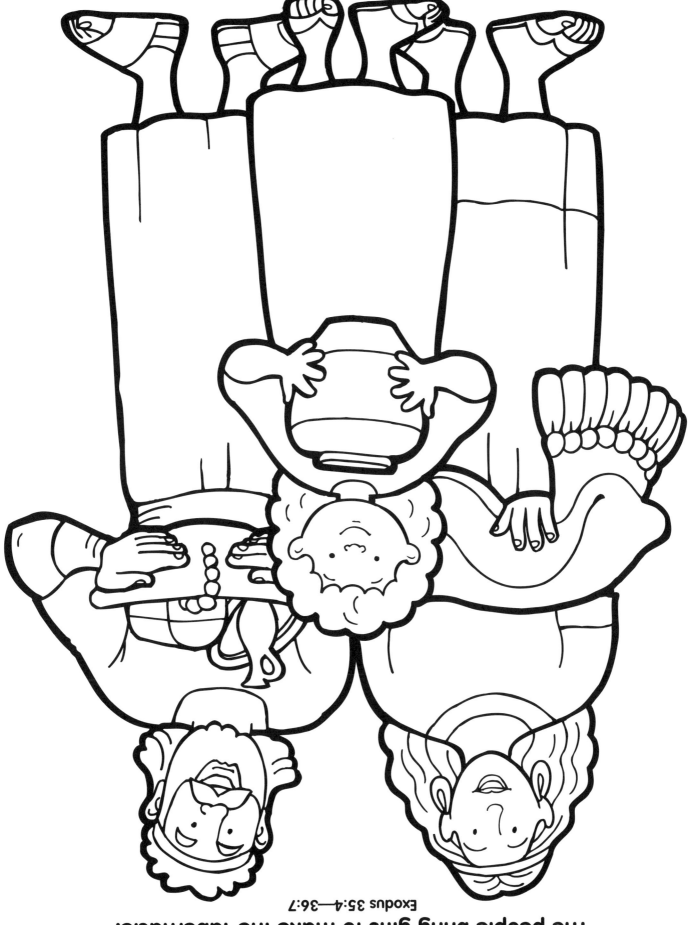

The people bring gifts to make the Tabernacle.
Exodus 35:4—36:7

The people bring gifts to make the Tabernacle.

Exodus 35:4—36:7

God gave Moses plans to make a tent church called a Tabernacle. The Tabernacle was to be a special place to worship God. Moses told the people exactly how it should be made.

All the people who wanted to brought gifts of gold, precious stones and other things that were needed to make the Tabernacle. The people brought more and more beautiful things! It seemed that everyone wanted to give their very best things to help make the Tabernacle!

Soon there was enough to make the Tabernacle, but the people kept bringing more gifts. Finally, the men in charge of working on the Tabernacle went to see Moses. They said, "Tell the people to stop bringing gifts. We have too much!"

The people made the Tabernacle just as God told them.

Spies visit the Promised Land.
Numbers 13—14:35

Spies visit the Promised Land.

Numbers 13—14:35

Moses sent 12 men to explore the land God promised to give the Israelite people. The men secretly looked at the cities and towns. They saw the good food that grew in the land. They saw the people who lived there.

The 12 men came back to Moses. They brought some of the fruit from the Promised Land—a bunch of grapes so big that two men had to carry it! But 10 of the men were scared. They told Moses that the people who lived in the land were too big and strong. They said the cities were too big. They did not think God could help them live in the land.

But two of the men, Joshua and Caleb, knew God would keep His promise to give them the land. "Don't be afraid," they said. "The Lord is with us." But the Israelites didn't believe Joshua and Caleb.

God told Moses that because these people did not trust Him, they would not be able to go to the Promised Land for a long time. The people would have to live in the desert for many more years. But God promised Joshua and Caleb would get to live in the Promised Land because they trusted God.

God provides water from a rock.

Numbers 20:1-13

God provides water from a rock.

Numbers 20:1-13

The people were thirsty. They came to Moses. "Why did you make us come out here to the desert?" they said. "Why did you make us leave Egypt? There is nothing good to eat here. There is no water."

Moses was angry with the people. They blamed him for all their problems. They forgot how God protected them and always cared for them. So Moses talked to God. God told Moses to speak to a rock in front of the people. God would make water come out of the rock.

Moses went to the rock. But Moses was so angry, he didn't do what God said. Instead of speaking to the rock, Moses hit the rock with his staff! God made water come out of the rock even though Moses didn't do what God said. God was sad that Moses didn't obey Him.

Moses asks God for help.
Numbers 21:4-9

Moses asks God for help.

Numbers 21:4-9

The Israelites were traveling through the desert. They kept complaining. They were tired. They were hungry. They were thirsty! The people forgot to thank God for the way He had helped them in the past.

The people complained more and more! Finally, God let poisonous snakes come into their camp. The snakes bit people. Some people died.

The Israelites came to Moses and said, "We sinned when we complained against God. Please tell God we are sorry. Please ask Him to take away the snakes."

Moses prayed. Then God told Moses what to do to help the people. Moses made a special pole and put a snake made of metal on the top of the pole. When the people looked at the pole, God would make them well. Once again, God had helped the Israelites out of trouble as they traveled to the Promised Land.

God's people remember crossing the river.

Joshua 4

God's people remember crossing the river.

Joshua 4

God's people were amazed! They were standing in the land that God had promised to give them long ago. They had traveled for years across the desert. God had led them all the way! And God had stopped the rushing river, so they could cross safely on dry ground.

When all the people and animals had safely crossed to the other side, Joshua told 12 men to go back into the riverbed. He told them to pick up large stones.

The men went into the riverbed. Each man picked up a large smooth stone. They brought the stones back to where Joshua and all the people were standing. The priests followed the men out of the riverbed, and CRASH! All the water came pouring back down the river again, just as it had been. No one would have guessed that it had ever been dry.

Joshua piled the stones into a big stack near the river. Whenever the people saw the stones, it would remind them how God had helped them cross the river on dry ground and come to the land God had promised them.

Jericho's walls fall down.
Joshua 6:1-20

Jericho's walls fall down.

Joshua 6:1-20

Joshua and the Israelites were in the land God had promised them. They were camped outside the city of Jericho. All around the city there was a huge wall made of rocks. The people of Jericho closed the gates to their city. They did not let anyone in or out. They were afraid of the Israelites, but they felt safe behind their city's big wall.

God told Joshua that the Israelites would take over the city of Jericho. God told Joshua what to do. Joshua and the Israelites did just what God said.

All of the Israelite men marched in a long line near the city wall. Some of the priests marched with them. The priests carried the box that held God's laws. Other priests blew on horns as they marched. They marched one time all the way around the city wall. That's all they did for six days!

Then on the seventh day, the Israelites marched around the wall seven times. Then they stopped. The priests blew the longest, loudest blasts they could make on their horns. And Joshua led the people to shout with loud voices!

As the Israelites shouted, CRASH! The wall around the city fell flat to the ground! The Israelites marched straight into the city. God had helped the Israelites take over Jericho, just as God had promised.

Joshua is tricked.
Joshua 9

Joshua is tricked.

Joshua 9

When Joshua led the Israelites into the Promised Land, other people were already living there. Many of these people and their kings wanted to fight against the Israelites. But one group of people, the Gibeonites, knew that God was helping the Israelites. They knew they could not win a fight against God! So they made up a plan to trick the Israelites.

Some of the Gibeonite men dressed up in worn-out, dirty clothes. They put on old sandals with holes in the bottoms. They packed dried-out moldy bread into old, cracked leather bags for their tired-looking donkeys to carry. Then they walked over to the Israelite camp.

The men told the Israelites they had come from a faraway country and wanted to be their friends.

Joshua and his helpers looked at the Gibeonites' old sandals and moldy bread. Joshua thought the Gibeonites were telling the truth. He forgot to ask God what to do. He agreed to be friends with the Gibeonites. Joshua promised that the Israelites would not fight against them.

But three days later Joshua found out the Gibeonites were really their neighbors! He angrily marched the Israelite army over to their camp. Joshua told them he would keep his promise. Israel would not fight against the Gibeonites, but the Gibeonites must become the Israelites' workers. The Gibeonites agreed. After all, it was easier to be helpers than to fight against an army helped by God!

God makes the sun stand still.
Joshua 10:1-15

God makes the sun stand still.

Joshua 10:1-15

Five kings who lived in the Promised Land had heard that the Gibeonites and Israelites made a promise to be friends. That made them angry. The kings decided to attack the Gibeonites. The Gibeonites were surprised. The Gibeonites needed help, quickly! They sent a messenger to Joshua and asked for his help.

Joshua had promised to help the Gibeonites, so he called for his army. The army began marching to Gibeon. They marched all night! As they marched, God told Joshua that they would win the battle.

The next morning the enemy armies woke up. They were surprised to see Joshua and his army.

The enemies tried to run away, but God sent hail that stopped them. But there were still more enemies, and the sun was going down soon.

So Joshua prayed. He said, "Let the sun stand still! Give us extra daylight until we win this fight." And that's exactly what happened. God stopped the sun from going down. At bedtime, the sun STILL hadn't gone down! The sun didn't go down until the Israelites had won the fight. God had helped the Israelites in an amazing way. No other day has ever been that long!

Deborah helps people obey God.
Judges 4:1-16

Deborah helps people obey God.

Judges 4:1-16

Deborah loved God and listened to Him. God told Deborah messages to give to His people. Many people came to talk to Deborah. She helped the people know how to obey God.

One day God gave Deborah a message for a man named Barak. Deborah told Barak, "God has an important job for you. He wants you to take 10,000 men to Mount Tabor. There you will fight the enemy Sisera and his army. And you will win!"

Barak was afraid when he heard this message. Sisera's army was big and had 900 strong chariots. Barak said, "Deborah, I will only go if you go with me." Deborah wanted Barak to trust God and obey, so she said she would go.

Soon 10,000 men marched with Barak and Deborah up Mount Tabor. Sisera was getting

ready to fight, too. He was sure he would win. After all, he had 900 strong, fast chariots! But Sisera didn't know the Israelites had God's help!

The Israelites camped on Mount Tabor, above a wide flat valley. Soon they saw Sisera and his army coming with all their chariots. As Barak and his men started down the mountain, God sent a thunderstorm! Lightning flashed. Rain poured. The chariots could go very fast on dry ground, but the rain turned the ground into mud! Those 900 strong chariots were STUCK. Sisera and his men ran away from their chariots. Barak's army chased them until there was no one left to chase! God had done what He said He would do! Everyone praised God!

An angel talks to Gideon.
Judges 6:1-24

An angel talks to Gideon.

Judges 6:1-24

The Midianites were the Israelites' enemies. They stole everything from the Israelites! The Israelites were so afraid they hid in caves in the mountains. The Israelites asked God to help them.

One day an Israelite named Gideon was hiding from the Midianites. Gideon was hiding because he didn't want the Midianites to come and steal the wheat he was threshing.

Suddenly an angel appeared and said, "The Lord is with you, mighty warrior." What a funny way to talk to someone who was hiding!

God told Gideon to save Israel from the Midianites. Gideon didn't think that he could save Israel, but God said that He would go with Gideon and help him. Gideon still wasn't sure, so he asked the angel to prove he was speaking from God. The angel did! After that, Gideon did what the angel told him to do.

God helps
Gideon
defeat the
Midianites.
Judges 7:1-21

God helps Gideon defeat the Midianites.

Judges 7:1-21

Many people came to help Gideon fight the Midianites. But many of the men were afraid. "Let everyone who is afraid go home," God told Gideon. Most of the men left.

But God thought Gideon's army was still too big. God told Gideon to take the men to the river to get a drink. Most of the men got down on their knees to drink. God told Gideon to send those men home.

Now only three hundred men were left. That was not very many! The army from Midian had more men than Gideon could count. There was no way that only three hundred men could win a battle against such a big army!

God told Gideon what to do. Gideon gave each man in his army a trumpet and a jar with a torch inside. The men surrounded the Midianite camp.

At just the right time they blew their trumpets, broke their jars and shouted, "The sword of the Lord and Gideon!" When the big Midianite army heard the noise and saw the lights, they ran away! God saved His people with a small army and a leader who obeyed God.

Samson is strong.

Judges 13:1-25; 16:1-22

Samson is strong.

Judges 13:1-25; 16:1-22

An angel told a man and woman that they were going to have a special baby. The angel told them that this baby should serve God all his life. The angel gave them special rules for this baby to follow. One of the rules was that he should never cut his hair.

The baby's name was Samson. After Samson was born, God helped him grow up strong. Samson fought the Philistines, who were hurting the Israelites. Samson became so strong that he could defeat entire armies by himself! Samson could break thick ropes as if they were strings and kill lions with his bare hands.

One day Samson let a woman called Delilah trick him. He told her how to make his strength go away. While Samson slept, Delilah called to the Philistines. She told them to cut off Samson's hair. When Samson's hair was cut, Samson woke up. Samson thought that he would still be strong, but the strength that God gave him was gone because he didn't obey God. The Philistines took him as their prisoner.

Ruth cares for Naomi.

Ruth 1—4

Naomi and her family were from Israel. Because there hadn't been enough food in Israel, they went to live in a country called Moab. Naomi's sons grew up and got married. One of them was married to a woman named Ruth.

After a while, Naomi's sons died. Her husband died, too. Naomi wanted to go back to Israel. Ruth said she would go with her. Ruth told Naomi, "I will go wherever you go. Your people will be my people and your God will be my God."

When Ruth and Naomi got to Israel, they didn't have any food. They needed some grain to make bread to eat. So Ruth went to a field where some workers were harvesting grain. She picked up the grain the workers left behind. It was hard work! And it took her a long time to gather enough grain for food.

A man named Boaz owned the field where Ruth picked up grain. Boaz was very kind to Ruth. He invited her to eat lunch with his workers. He told his workers to help Ruth by leaving lots of extra grain for her to find.

Ruth brought the grain to Naomi to be made into bread. Naomi was glad Ruth worked hard so that they could have food to eat. Ruth and Naomi were thankful that Boaz was so kind. Ruth even married Boaz! God took care of Ruth and Naomi.

God answers Hannah's prayer.

1 Samuel 1:1—2:11

God answers Hannah's prayer.

1 Samuel 1:1—2:11

Hannah's husband had another wife named Peninnah. Peninnah had sons and daughters, but Hannah didn't have any children. Peninnah made fun of Hannah because she didn't have children. Hannah felt sad.

When Hannah's family went to worship God at the Tabernacle, Hannah cried and cried. She prayed, "Please God, give me a son."

Eli, the priest, saw Hannah praying and thought she was drunk. He told Hannah to stop getting drunk. Hannah said, "I am not drunk. I am very sad and am asking God to help me." Eli told her to go in peace. Eli asked God to give her what she asked for.

God answered Hannah's prayer. Hannah named her baby boy Samuel. When he was old enough, Hannah took Samuel to the Tabernacle so that he could serve God.

God speaks to Samuel.
1 Samuel 3:1-21

God speaks to Samuel.

1 Samuel 3:1-21

Eli, the priest, was getting old. Samuel helped Eli take care of the Tabernacle. Samuel slept on a mat on the floor of the Tabernacle. One night Samuel heard a voice calling his name. Samuel jumped up and ran to where Eli was sleeping. "Here I am. You called me."

Eli said, "I didn't call you. Go back to sleep." Samuel went back to his mat on the floor. Soon, Samuel heard the voice again. Samuel quickly ran to Eli again, but Eli hadn't called him. Samuel went back to his mat again. But he heard the voice again! Samuel thought it had to be Eli calling! There was no one else who would call him in the middle of the night. Samuel ran to Eli. Eli realized that God was calling Samuel. God must have something important to tell Samuel.

Eli told Samuel to go back and lie down. Eli said, "If He calls you, say 'Speak, Lord, for your servant is listening.'" Samuel did what Eli said. God told Samuel what He was going to do. Samuel listened to God.

Samuel chooses a king.
1 Samuel 8:1—10:24

Samuel chooses a king.

1 Samuel 8:1—10:24

Samuel grew up to be the leader of Israel. He was called a judge. Now Samuel was getting old. Some people talked to Samuel. They said, "Give us a king like all the other countries around us. We want to be like them."

Samuel was upset because he knew God was the real King of Israel! So he prayed to God. God said, "Samuel, warn them. Tell them that a king will make them his servants and will take their land and animals."

Samuel told the people all the things God had said. The people didn't care! They said, "We want a king anyway!"

About that time, a young man named Saul was out looking for his father's lost donkeys. As Saul walked into town, Samuel saw Saul. God said, "Samuel, here's the man I want to be king."

Samuel said to Saul, "I'd like you to come and eat with me. And don't worry, your donkeys have been found." The next morning, Samuel took a small bottle of olive oil and poured it on Saul's head saying, "The Lord has chosen you to be the leader of His people." And from that time, God helped Saul become ready to be king.

Saul disobeys God.
1 Samuel 15

Saul disobeys God.

1 Samuel 15

One day, God gave Samuel a message for King Saul. Samuel told Saul, "God will help you win your battle against the enemy. But God says that after the battle, you must get rid of every-thing that belongs to the enemy. You may not keep anything!"

Saul led the Israelite army into battle. They won, just as God had said they would. But Saul decided to bring home some of the best cattle and sheep. He disobeyed God's command! God told Samuel what Saul had done. Samuel went to meet Saul as he was returning from the battle. Behind Saul, there were the cows and sheep walking along, mooing and baaing! They showed that Saul had disobeyed God.

Saul made many excuses about why he had disobeyed God. But Samuel told Saul that nothing is more important than obeying God. Samuel told Saul, "Because you didn't obey God, you will not be king much longer."

As Samuel walked away, Saul grabbed his robe to stop him. A piece of the robe tore off. Samuel said, "Just like you tore a piece from my robe, God has torn the kingdom from you. God doesn't lie or change His mind!" Saul was sorry, but he couldn't change what he had done. God still loved Saul, but He was not going to let Saul be king for much longer.

David is chosen as king.

1 Samuel 16:1-13

God had said that King Saul would not be king much longer. God told Samuel to go to the man God had chosen to be the new king. "Go to the town of Bethlehem. Find a man named Jesse. I have chosen one of Jesse's sons to be the king."

Samuel obeyed God and went to Bethlehem. He talked to Jesse. He looked at each of Jesse's seven sons. The oldest son was tall and strong. *Surely this is the one God wants to be king,* thought Samuel.

"No," God said to Samuel, "he is not the one. You can only see how he looks on the outside. But I have chosen a man who loves Me and will obey Me. That cannot be seen from the outside."

So Samuel looked at the next son. But God said he wasn't the one either. One after another, Jesse's seven sons walked by. But none of them was the one God had picked! Finally Samuel asked Jesse, "Do you have any MORE sons?"

Jesse told him that his youngest son, David, was out taking care of the sheep. Samuel asked to see him. When David walked in, God said, "This is the one I have chosen." So Samuel took out a little animal horn filled with oil. Samuel poured some oil on David's head to show that he was the one God had chosen to be the next king. God had chosen David because he knew David loved God with all his heart.

David plays his harp for King Saul.
1 Samuel 16:14-23

David plays his harp for King Saul.

1 Samuel 16:14-23

King Saul sat on his throne. He didn't want to talk to anyone. He didn't want to do anything. King Saul felt sad. The king's servants were worried. They wanted to make the king feel better. What could the servants do? What might make the king feel better?

"Maybe some music would help," one of the servants said.

Another servant said, "There is a shepherd boy named David who is a good musician. He is a brave and handsome young man. He loves God. David could play his harp for the king."

King Saul sent a messenger to David's father. "Send David here so he can work for me." David's father sent David to King Saul. Whenever King Saul felt sad, David played the harp for him. Then King Saul would feel better

David fights Goliath.

1 Samuel 17:1-58

David fights Goliath.

1 Samuel 17:1-58

David's brothers were in Saul's army. One day, David's father sent him to visit his brothers. David saw the army getting ready to fight the Philistines. Suddenly, a giant Philistine came out. Saul's army was afraid. They ran back to their tents.

Goliath, the Philistine giant, was more than nine feet tall. Goliath yelled, "Choose a man to fight me. If he is able to kill me, we will become your slaves. But if I win the fight, you will become our slaves." No one in the Israelite camp wanted to fight Goliath. They didn't think anyone could beat someone so big!

David knew that God was stronger than Goliath. David said, "I'll go and fight him." King Saul heard what David said. "You're too young and small to fight Goliath," King Saul said.

"But God helped me fight lions and bears when I took care of my father's sheep, and God will help me now," David answered.

Goliath laughed when he saw David. He even made fun of God! David used just his slingshot and a stone to fight Goliath. God helped David save his people from the Philistine army.

David and Jonathan are friends.

1 Samuel 18:1-4; 20:1-42

David and Jonathan are friends.

1 Samuel 18:1-4; 20:1-42

"Hooray for David!" All the women danced and sang, "David is a great warrior!" Everyone loved David. Even King Saul's son, Prince Jonathan, liked David. Jonathan knew that David loved God, and that David was a brave warrior. Jonathan wanted David to be his good friend. Jonathan gave David some gifts. David and Jonathan even promised to remain good friends whatever happened in the future.

King Saul made David an officer in the army. Whenever the king sent David on a mission, David did a great job. God always helped David. But King Saul was not happy. King Saul was jealous of David. Saul was afraid that his people would want David to be king instead!

David found out that the king wanted to hurt him, so David ran away and hid. Later he talked to Jonathan. Jonathan and David were very sad. Jonathan helped David get away from King Saul. David promised to always be kind to Jonathan and his children.

David doesn't hurt Saul.

1 Samuel 24:1-22

David doesn't hurt Saul.

1 Samuel 24:1-22

King Saul and his men chased David. David and his men quietly hid in the back of a deep dark cave. They didn't say a word. Saul and his men were right outside the cave! They didn't know where David was.

King Saul went inside the cave by himself. He thought the cave was empty.

Inside the cave, David's men said, "Now you can stop King Saul from chasing you. You can kill him and become king."

David crept up next to King Saul. David cut off the corner of King Saul's robe. David didn't hurt the king. King Saul didn't even know that David was there.

After King Saul left the cave, David came out and called to him. David showed the king the corner of the robe that David had cut off. David said, "Why are you chasing me? I have not done anything wrong." King Saul felt sorry for being mean to David. King Saul stopped chasing David for a while.

Abigail is wise.

1 Samuel 25:2-42

The Really Big Book of Bible Story Coloring Pages • 105

Abigail is wise.

1 Samuel 25:2-42

David and his men lived in the desert. A man named Nabal lived there, too. Nabal had many sheep and goats. Every day the sheep and the goats ate grass and drank water near the place where David and his men were. David's men could have stolen some of them. But instead, David and his men made sure that everything Nabal had stayed safe.

One day David sent some of his men to see Nabal. Nabal should have given them some of his food to tell David thank you for being kind to him. Nabal didn't give them anything. Nabal even said very bad things about David!

David was angry. David and his men got ready to go hurt Nabal. Nabal's wife, Abigail, heard what happened. Abigail gathered lots of food. She quickly put the food on some donkeys. Abigail and her servants went to meet David. "I'm sorry. I didn't see the men you sent," Abigail said. "Don't pay any attention to what Nabal said. He was wrong."

David was glad Abigail kept him from doing something mean when he felt angry. David thanked God for Abigail.

David brings the Ark to Jerusalem.
2 Samuel 6:1-19; 1 Chronicles 15:25—16:3

David brings the Ark to Jerusalem.

2 Samuel 6:1-19; 1 Chronicles 15:25—16:3

The Ark of the Covenant was a beautiful box God had told the Israelites to make from gold and wood. The Ark showed the people that God was always with them. Only the priests could carry the Ark. They used special poles, so they didn't touch the Ark itself. No one was to touch the Ark.

But the Ark had been left out in the country. Now that David was king, he wanted to bring the Ark to Jerusalem. David and some of his men put the Ark on a wagon that was pulled by oxen. They didn't carry it on poles as God had said to do. As they were walking, one of the oxen stumbled. A man touched the Ark to keep it from falling. When he touched the Ark, he fell to the ground dead.

Everyone was sad! Even though the man was trying to help, he had disobeyed God's command

not to touch the ark. David and his men left the Ark at a nearby house.

Later, David took his men and again went to bring the Ark to Jerusalem. This time they obeyed God's rules exactly. The priests carried the Ark on poles. King David led the big crowd of people. He sang and danced to show how glad he was that God was with His people. The people were singing and playing cymbals, harps and trumpets. Everyone wanted God to know how happy they were to have the Ark in Jerusalem!

When the Ark was safely placed in a special tent, David gave gifts to God and prayed. David finished the wonderful day of celebration by giving gifts to everyone who came to celebrate.

King Solomon is wise.

1 Kings 3:1-15

King Solomon is wise.

1 Kings 3:1-15

Solomon was the new king. Solomon knew that it would not be easy to be a good and fair king. He knew that he needed God to help him. King Solomon went to a special place to worship God.

That night, while Solomon was sleeping, he had a dream. In his dream, God told Solomon to ask for whatever he wanted. Solomon didn't ask for money. He didn't ask for a long life. He didn't even ask to become famous. Solomon asked God to make him wise so he could be a good king.

God was happy that Solomon asked for wisdom. God knew that Solomon was more concerned about doing what was right than about getting rich. God made a promise to Solomon. "Since you asked for wisdom and not for long life or money," God said, "I will make you more wise than anyone else. I will also give you riches and honor." The Bible says Solomon was the wisest person who ever lived.

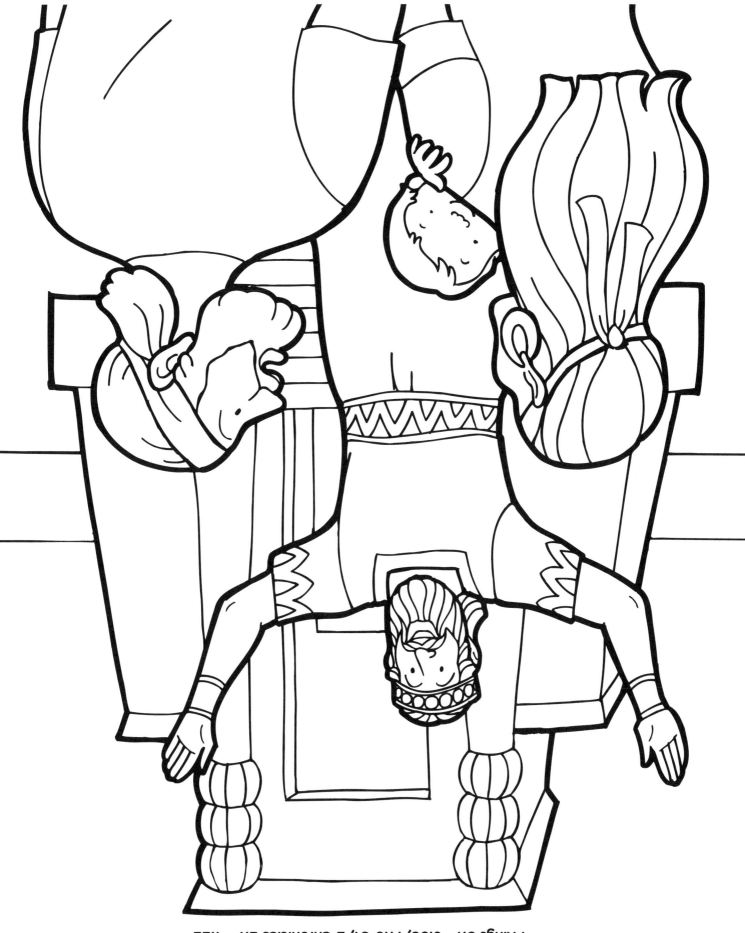

Solomon builds the Temple.
1 Kings 5:1—6:38, 7:13-51; 2 Chronicles 2:1—4:22

Solomon builds the Temple.

1 Kings 5:1—6:38; 7:13-51; 2 Chronicles 2:1—4:22

King Solomon wanted to build a Temple for God. The Temple would be a place for people to come to pray and learn about God. King Solomon hired many people to work on the Temple. There were people who carried wood, people who cut giant stones, people who carved beautiful designs in the wood, and even people who put pure gold over everything!

King Solomon also had skilled craftsmen make many beautiful gold and bronze things to put in the Temple. There were tables and lampstands, dishes and pillars, stands and basins. It was a wonderful Temple! Inside, everything glittered with gold. From the outside, you could see giant pillars and beautiful decorations.

After everything was finished, King Solomon called all the people of Israel to come to the Temple. They all thanked God and had a big celebration.

Solomon worships idols.
1 Kings 11:1-13,28-40

Solomon worships idols.

1 Kings 11:1-13,28-40

Solomon was the king of Israel. He was the wisest man who ever lived. But as wise as Solomon was, he disobeyed God. First, he married a princess from Egypt. She brought statues of false gods with her and worshiped them in Solomon's house. Then Solomon married more and more foreign princesses. They brought their statues and idols with them, too.

For years, Solomon's wives told him to worship these false gods. After a while, Solomon began to do what his wives said to do. Solomon even prayed to these statues because he thought they had some sort of power. Solomon disobeyed God.

God told Solomon, "You know that I have always said to worship only Me. You have disobeyed Me. After you die, I am going to divide your kingdom in two. Your son will be king over only a small part. One of your servants will be king over the biggest part." God's words made Solomon sad. But he still disobeyed God and did not ask God to forgive him.

One day, Solomon's servant Jeroboam was walking on a road. He met a prophet who showed God's message to Jeroboam. The prophet ripped Jeroboam's coat into 12 pieces. He told Jeroboam to take 10 of the pieces because he would rule most of Solomon's kingdom. Solomon heard what happened and did another foolish thing—he tried to kill Jeroboam! Even though Solomon was the wisest man who ever lived, he stopped being wise when he stopped obeying God and loving Him more than anything else.

God sends
ravens with
food for Elijah.
1 Kings 17:1-6

God sends ravens with food for Elijah.
1 Kings 17:1-6

Ahab was the new king of Israel. Ahab didn't worship God. Ahab built places to worship idols instead of God. Many of the people in Israel stopped worshiping God because of the evil things that Ahab did. God was angry with Ahab.

Elijah didn't worship idols. Elijah obeyed God. Elijah went to see King Ahab. "There won't be any rain for a long time," Elijah said. "There won't be any rain to make the food in the fields grow. There won't be any rain to make the grass green. There won't be any rain to give the people water to drink." Ahab was very angry.

So God told Elijah to hide from the king. Elijah left the city. He walked and walked. Elijah came to a brook. Elijah drank some water from the brook. God told Elijah to stay by the brook. God told Elijah that birds called ravens were going to bring food to him. Every morning and every evening the ravens came with bread and meat for Elijah to eat.

God helps Elijah and a widow.
1 Kings 17:7-16

God helps Elijah and a widow.

1 Kings 17:7-16

In the land of the Israelites there had not been any rain for a long time. God had helped the prophet Elijah have enough food and water. But soon the brook near Elijah dried up. God told Elijah to go to a certain town. God said that a woman who lived in that town would give Elijah food.

Elijah walked to the town. Near the town gate, Elijah saw a woman picking up sticks. Elijah asked the woman to bring him some water to drink. As the woman left to get water, Elijah called, "And could you please bring me some bread?"

"Oh, I'm sorry!" the woman told him. "I have only enough flour and oil to make a little bread for my son and me. It's all the food we have left. After this we will die."

"Don't worry," Elijah said kindly. "Make a little bread for me first. Then make some for you and your son. God has promised that there will be enough food for all of us until it rains again!" The woman did what Elijah asked. She mixed some flour and oil and patted it out flat. After it baked on the fire, she gave it to Elijah.

Then she began to make bread for her son and herself. She went to get the last bit of flour from the flour jar. She looked in the jar. There was still flour in it! Then she peeked into the oil pitcher. The pitcher still had oil in it! There was enough flour and oil to make all the bread they needed for supper!

And every day after that, the jar of flour and the pitcher of oil were never empty until there was food in the country again. The woman, her son and Elijah must have thanked God many times!

God answers Elijah's prayer.
1 Kings 18:16-39

God answers Elijah's prayer.

1 Kings 18:16-39

Many Israelites stopped worshiping God. They worshiped idols instead. Elijah said, "How long will you do this? Worship the one true God!" But the people didn't listen.

Elijah challenged the prophets of Baal (a false god) to have a contest. Elijah said, "The God who sends fire from heaven is the real God." The people thought the contest was a good idea. They wanted to see whether God or Baal could send fire from heaven.

The prophets of Baal began asking Baal to send fire. They danced and prayed. Baal could not send fire. Baal was not God. Baal was an idol the people made. He couldn't do anything.

Then it was Elijah's turn. First Elijah repaired an old altar where people used to worship the one true God. Elijah dug a trench around the altar. Elijah had some men pour lots of water on the altar. Elijah prayed. God sent fire from heaven. The fire burned up everything that was on the altar. The fire even burned up all the water the men had poured on the altar. Now the people knew who the real God was. The people worshiped God.

Elisha becomes a prophet.
1 Kings 19:19-21

Elisha becomes a prophet.

1 Kings 19:19-21

When Elijah finished God's work, God said that a man named Elisha was going to be the next prophet. So Elijah went on his way to find Elisha. Elijah wanted to teach Elisha how to do God's work.

Elijah found Elisha plowing in his father's field. Elisha was walking behind a pair of oxen.

Elijah walked up behind Elisha and threw his cloak around Elisha's shoulders. He did this to show that God had chosen Elisha to learn from him and follow him.

Now Elisha knew that he would be a prophet. He went home to say good-bye to his parents. He also made a big meal to celebrate his leaving home. Then Elisha went with Elijah to help him and to learn about obeying God by being a prophet.

•

Elijah goes to heaven.
2 Kings 2:1-14

Elijah goes to heaven.

2 Kings 2:1-14

Elijah was an important prophet who told people messages from God. But it was time for Elijah to leave and go to heaven. Elijah and Elisha walked together. They crossed a river. Elijah said, "If God lets you see me when I go up to heaven, then you will take over my job."

Suddenly a chariot and some horses that looked like fire swooped down out of the sky! Then Elijah went to heaven in a whirlwind. All that was left was Elijah's cloak that had fallen to the ground. Elisha picked up the cloak.

Elisha had seen the chariot and the horses. It was very exciting! Elisha was sad that Elijah was not going to be with him anymore, but now Elisha had an important job to do. Elisha knew God was with him and would help him.

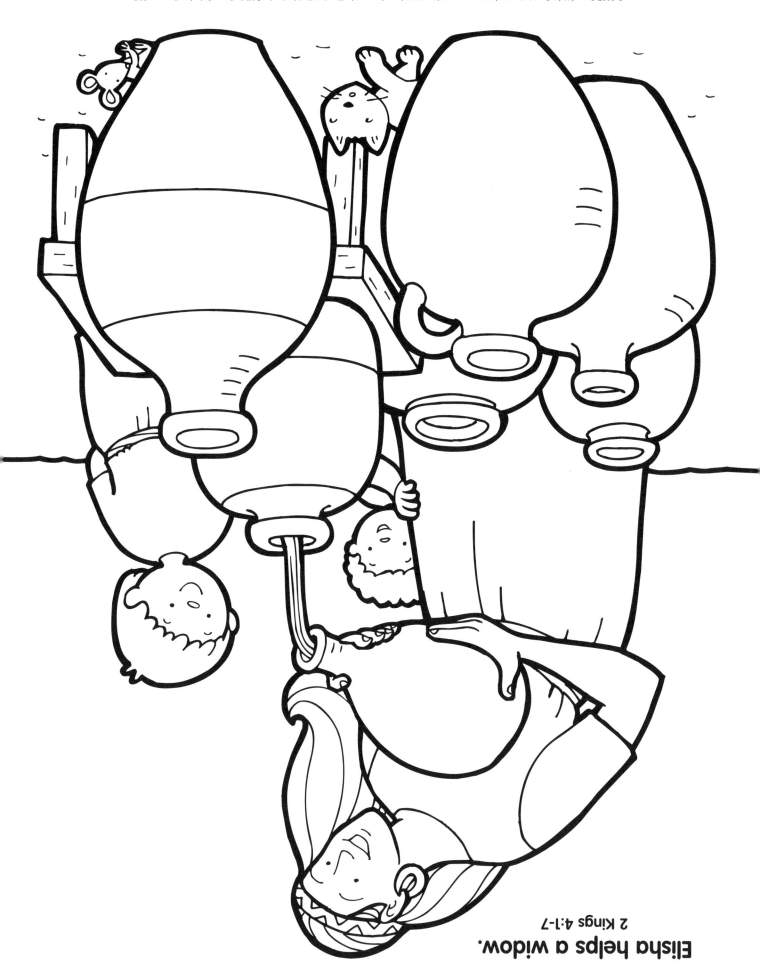

Elisha helps a widow.
2 Kings 4:1-7

Elisha helps a widow.

2 Kings 4:1-7

A woman's husband died. The woman had no money to pay her bills. The bill collector said, "Give me your two sons so I can sell them as slaves and get my money back."

The woman asked Elisha for help. Elisha asked, "What do you have in your house?" The woman said, "I don't have anything except a little oil."

"Go ask your neighbors to give you empty jars," Elisha said. "Get as many jars as you can. Then go inside your house and shut the door. Pour oil into all the jars." The woman and her sons did exactly what Elisha said.

The woman took her little jar of oil and began to pour oil into the jars. She filled up one jar, then another and another. She kept pouring oil until all the jars were full! When all the jars were full, the oil stopped flowing out of her jar. The woman knew that only God could fill all those jars with oil from her little jar!

Elisha told the woman to sell the jars of oil and use the money to pay what she owed. She did what Elisha told her to, and she even had some money left over!

Friends build a room for Elisha.

2 Kings 4:8-10

Friends build a room for Elisha.

2 Kings 4:8-10

Elisha was God's prophet. He went many places to tell people about God. In one town Elisha visited often, there was a kind lady and her husband. The lady and her husband were glad when Elisha visited their town. They always listened to Elisha tell about God. This lady often invited him to eat dinner with her and her husband.

One day the woman said to her husband, "I know Elisha loves God. I want to do something kind for him. Let's build a room on the roof of our house for him. We'll put a bed, a chair, a table and a lamp in the room. When Elisha comes to visit, he can eat with us and sleep in his own room."

The woman's husband thought it was a good idea. So they built Elisha a room. The woman and her husband moved the furniture into the room. It was just right! They could hardly wait until Elisha came back.

The next time Elisha came to the town he went to the woman's house. The woman said, "Come quickly, Elisha. We have something special to show you!" The woman and her husband walked with Elisha up the stairs to the roof of their home—and there was his new room! Elisha was very thankful! God cared for Elisha by giving him kind friends.

Elisha leads a blind army.
2 Kings 6:8-23

Elisha leads a blind army.

2 Kings 6:8-23

A king was angry with Elisha because Elisha helped the king's enemies. The king sent an army to capture Elisha. The army came at night. They surrounded the town where Elisha was sleeping. The army waited. In the morning, Elisha's servant saw the army. He was afraid. Elisha's servant said, "Oh, no! What will we do?"

"Don't be afraid," Elisha said. Elisha prayed for his servant. Then Elisha's servant saw horses and chariots that looked like fire all around the enemy army. Elisha's servant knew that God was taking care of them. Then Elisha prayed again. This time he prayed that God would make the enemy army blind.

Elisha led the blind army to the city where the king of Israel was. Then Elisha prayed that God would let the army see again. The men in the army looked and saw that they were trapped! The soldiers of Israel were all around them. Elisha said to the king of Israel, "Give these people food and water and then let them go back home." Elisha was kind to the army that came to capture him. The army stopped being mean to Elisha's people for a while.

Joash repairs the Temple.
2 Kings 12:1-15; 2 Chronicles 24:1-14

Joash repairs the Temple.

2 Kings 12:1-15; 2 Chronicles 24:1-14

No one cleaned up the Temple anymore. The Temple was dirty. Many things inside the Temple were broken. Some important things were missing. The walls and roof needed to be repaired.

King Joash wanted to fix the Temple. He told the priests to use the money that people brought to fix the Temple.

The priests put a large box by the altar so everyone could put money in it to help fix the Temple. Whenever the box got full, the priests would empty the box. They gave the money to the men who were fixing the Temple. The men worked hard and did their best. All the people wanted the Temple to look nice again. The people wanted to use the Temple to worship God and to learn more about Him.

Josiah hears God's Word.

2 Kings 22:1—23:3; 2 Chronicles 34:14-32

Josiah hears God's Word.

2 Kings 22:1—23:3; 2 Chronicles 34:14-32

Josiah was only eight years old when he became king. No one in his country read God's Word anymore. Even the priests who were in charge of the Temple didn't know where God's Word was!

One day a priest in the Temple found a scroll with God's Word written on it. He ran to the king's helper. "Here is a scroll with God's Word written on it!" the priest said. "King Josiah will want to see this!" The helper took the scroll to the king.

The king's helper read God's Word to Josiah. King Josiah listened to God's Word. King Josiah loved God and wanted to obey God's Word, but when he heard what was written in God's Word, he cried. It made him sad to learn that his people were not obeying God.

King Josiah called all the leaders together. He told them what God's Word said. Josiah and all the leaders promised to obey God's Word.

Hezekiah celebrates the Passover.

2 Chronicles 29—30

Hezekiah celebrates the Passover.

2 Chronicles 29—30

Hezekiah was now the king of Judah. His father had disobeyed God all of his life and worshiped false gods from other countries.

But Hezekiah did not want to be like his father. As soon as he became king, he talked to all the men whose families had served in the Temple and told them to get ready to serve God again. They opened the doors of the Temple and cleaned it, so everyone could come to worship God.

Hezekiah sent letters and messengers throughout Judah and Israel. He invited everyone to come to Jerusalem to celebrate Passover. Passover is a

holiday God's people celebrate to remember how God had helped the Israelites escape from slavery in Egypt. People were excited as they heard the news that they could worship God again in the Temple.

On the day Passover began, there was a large crowd of people in Jerusalem. For the first time in a long time, people from Israel and Judah worshiped God together. Everyone was so glad to celebrate God's goodness that they kept celebrating for another whole week!

Job talks with God.
Job 1—2:10; 42

Job talks with God.

Job 1—2:10; 42

A man named Job had some terrible things happen to him. A huge storm killed all his children, his animals were all stolen, and he had gotten very sick. Job was very sad. But God had not forgotten about Job. God still loved Job and cared for him. God talked to Job to help him understand how great God is and how much He cared about all His creation, including Job!

God said, "Tell me, Job, do you know how I made the earth? And do you know how I control the oceans and keep their waters from washing all over the land? Job, can you make the sun rise? Or can you make the rain fall and the grass grow for the animals to eat?"

Job thought about the world. He knew that he couldn't control the oceans or make the sun rise. He couldn't make food for the birds and animals. He couldn't make rain fall or grass grow. Then Job remembered God's love and power.

Job said to God, "I know you can do all things. Now I understand Your power and Your love. I'm sorry that I did not trust You."

Now Job trusted that God would do what was best. Later, God gave Job twice as many animals as he had before. God also gave Job more children. Job learned that he could trust God's love and power all the time!

Jonah disobeys God.

Jonah 1—2:10

Jonah disobeys God.

Jonah 1—2:10

God was not happy with the way the people in Nineveh acted. God told Jonah to warn the people in Nineveh that God would punish them for all the bad things they kept doing. But Jonah didn't like the people in Nineveh and didn't want them to get a warning. So Jonah decided to disobey God. Jonah got on a boat that was going the other way.

God wanted Jonah to obey Him. God sent a storm that made the boat start to sink. The people on the boat were afraid. Jonah said, "God sent this storm because I ran away from Him. If you want this storm to stop, you must throw me overboard." The people on the boat threw Jonah into the water. Suddenly, the sea was still.

Jonah went down, down, down. Jonah wanted to breathe, but he couldn't. Jonah saw a giant fish swimming toward him! Jonah tried to swim away, but the giant fish opened its giant mouth and swallowed Jonah. Gulp!

Jonah was in the belly of the big fish. Now Jonah could breathe. It must have been very smelly! Jonah was sorry he had disobeyed God. He prayed and promised to obey God. Finally, God made the fish swim to the shore and spit Jonah up on the beach.

Isaiah writes God's messages.

Isaiah 6:1-8; 9:1-7

The people and rulers of Israel were doing many wrong things. They were not obeying God's laws. But God never stopped loving His people. He sent people called prophets to tell His messages and warnings to the people.

One day God chose a man named Isaiah to be a prophet. Isaiah had a vision, like a dream, about being in heaven. God was sitting on a throne. Many angels were worshiping Him. Isaiah thought he was going to die because he had seen God. God is holy and Isaiah knew he could never be good enough to be in God's presence.

One of the angels touched Isaiah's lips with a burning coal. The angel explained that now Isaiah would be ready for the job God wanted him to do. Then Isaiah heard God ask, "Whom shall I send?" God wanted someone to tell people about Himself. Isaiah answered, "Here I am. Send me!"

So God gave Isaiah many messages to write down and tell the people. Even though Isaiah lived hundreds of years before Jesus was born, many of these messages were about Jesus! Isaiah told that Jesus was going to be a great King and that Jesus would die to take the punishment for our sins. Isaiah wrote down many more things that were going to happen. We can read about them in our Bible.

The king destroys the scroll of God's Words.

Jeremiah 36:1-32

The King destroys the scroll of God's Words.

Jeremiah 36:1-32

God told Jeremiah some things to write down. Jeremiah called his friend Baruch to write down the words God told Jeremiah. Baruch carefully wrote down everything Jeremiah told him.

Then Jeremiah told Baruch to take the scroll he had written on and read it in the Temple so all the people could hear God's words. Some men who worked for the king heard what Baruch read. They asked Baruch to give them the scroll. Then they told Baruch and Jeremiah to go and hide, because they knew the king would be angry when he heard God's words.

The men who worked for the king took the scroll and read it to the king. The king didn't want to hear what God said. The king cut up the scroll and threw it in the fire! The king tried to put Baruch and Jeremiah in jail, but God protected them. Then God told Jeremiah to tell Baruch to write the words down again. Those words are still in our Bible today!

Daniel and his friends choose to obey God.
Daniel 1:1-21

Daniel and his friends choose to obey God.

Daniel 1:1-21

Daniel and his friends were taken to a faraway palace. The king wanted them to learn to work for him. The king gave them some special food. Daniel and his friends knew that God did not want them to eat the kind of food that the king gave them.

Daniel and his friends wanted to obey God. Daniel asked the king's helper to give his friends and him only vegetables and water. The king's helper was afraid that Daniel and his friends would not be as healthy as some of the other boys who were learning to work for the king. The king's helper knew that the king would be angry if Daniel and his friends were not healthy.

Daniel said, "Please test us for ten days. Give us only vegetables and water and then see who is healthiest—my friends and I or the others." The king's helper agreed to test them.

After ten days, Daniel and his friends looked healthier than any of the other young men. God helped Daniel and his friends. The king liked Daniel and his friends. He gave them important jobs.

God protects Daniel's friends in a furnace.

Daniel 3:1-30

God protects Daniel's friends in a furnace.

Daniel 3:1-30

King Nebuchadnezzar built a tall, tall statue. King Nebuchadnezzar wanted everyone to bow down and worship his statue. The king said, "Anyone who does not bow down will be thrown into a blazing furnace!"

Some men who worked for the king saw that Shadrach, Meshach and Abednego did not bow down to the king's statue. They did not bow down because they knew they should only worship God, not a statue.

The king was very angry with the three men. The king ordered his guards to tie up Shadrach, Meshach and Abednego and throw them into the hottest furnace. But when they were in the furnace, the king saw something very strange. Shadrach, Meshach and Abednego were not being burned up! They were not even tied up anymore. They were walking around inside the furnace with another person—an angel!

The king called to Shadrach, Meshach and Abednego, "Servants of the Most High God, come out!" The king said, "Praise God who sent an angel to save His servants. Shadrach, Meshach and Abednego would rather give up their lives than worship any god other than the one true God."

Daniel explains the handwriting on the wall.
Daniel 5

Daniel explains the handwriting on the wall.

Daniel 5

Belshazzar was the new king of Babylon. He liked to have parties. At one party, King Belshazzar used some beautiful gold cups. These cups had been stolen from God's Temple in Jerusalem. But the king did not care that these cups belonged to God. He didn't love or obey God.

During this party a huge hand suddenly appeared. The finger of the hand began writing words on the wall. The king was very afraid as he watched the hand. None of the king's helpers could tell what the words meant.

Then the queen remembered a wise man named Daniel. The king told his servants to bring Daniel to him. The king asked Daniel to tell him what the writing meant. Daniel said the words meant that God had seen how the king had disobeyed. Soon his time as king would be over. Someone else would take his place.

That very night, another man came and took over the city. He became the new king of Babylon. God's warning came true!

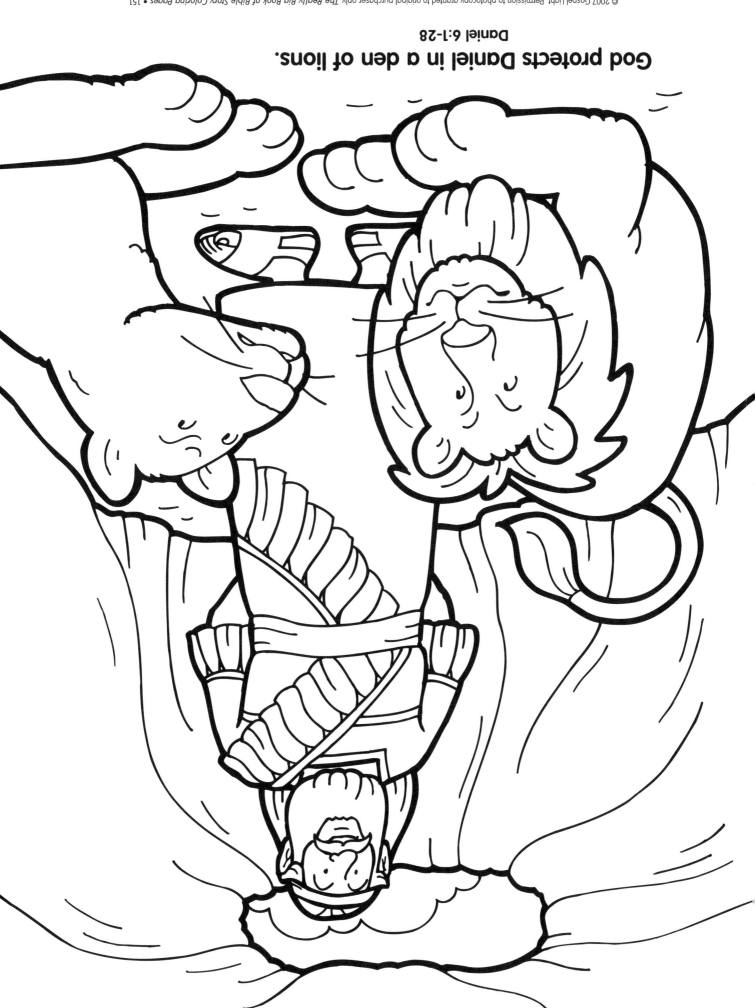

God protects Daniel in a den of lions.

Daniel 6:1-28

God protects Daniel in a den of lions.

Daniel 6:1-28

Daniel loved God and prayed to Him every day. In fact, he prayed three times every day. Daniel knew that praying to God was a right thing to do.

There were some mean men who did not like Daniel. They went to the king and said, "King, we think you should make a rule that everyone must pray only to you. If people pray to anyone else but you, they will be thrown into a cave filled with lions!" The king thought this was a good idea.

The next day Daniel prayed to God. The mean men watched as Daniel prayed to God. Then they ran to tell the king what they saw.

The king was sad. Daniel was his friend. The king knew he had been tricked into hurting Daniel. But the king had to obey the rule, too. Daniel was put into a big cave where hungry lions lived.

All night the king worried about Daniel. The next morning, the king ran to the lions' cave. He called, "Daniel! Daniel!" Daniel called out, "King, I am safe. The Lord God took care of me!"

The king was so glad that Daniel was not hurt. Then the king told everyone what God had done.

Esther is chosen queen.
Esther 2:1-18

Esther is chosen queen.

Esther 2:1-18

The queen didn't do what King Xerxes wanted. The king was very angry. "What should I do?" the king asked his friends.

The king's friends said, "Send her away and find a new queen." So the king started looking for a new queen. Many beautiful girls in the kingdom were brought to the palace.

One girl who was brought to the palace was named Esther. Esther was very beautiful. Esther met the king. The king liked Esther. The king said, "I want Esther to be the new queen." The king put a crown on Esther's head. The king invited many people to a banquet for Queen Esther. The king was so happy that he told everyone to take a holiday. The king didn't know that God had a special job for Esther to do.

Queen Esther saves her people.
Esther 4:1—7:10

Queen Esther saves her people.

Esther 4:1—7:10

Haman had an evil plan. He tricked King Xerxes into making a law to kill all the Jewish people. The king and Haman didn't know that Queen Esther was Jewish. Queen Esther had to ask the king to save her people.

It was against the law for anyone to go to the king unless he wanted to see that person. Queen Esther was afraid the king would be angry with her, so she asked all her people to pray and stop eating for three days. After three days, Esther went to see the king. The king was happy to see her!

Queen Esther invited the king to a banquet. She also invited Haman. After two banquets, Esther asked the king to save her people. The king was angry. He asked, "Who wanted to hurt my queen?"

"It's Haman," Esther answered. The king let Esther write a new law to protect Jewish people. The king gave everything Haman owned to Esther and had Haman put to death. The Jews were saved!

Nehemiah rebuilds the walls.

Nehemiah 2:11—4:23

Nehemiah rebuilds the walls.

Nehemiah 2:11—4:23

Nehemiah was the king's special helper. One day, Nehemiah's brother came from far away to visit him. "The city where we used to live had strong walls. Now they are broken. The city is not safe."

Nehemiah was sad. So Nehemiah prayed to God.

When the king saw Nehemiah he asked him, "Why are you so sad?" Nehemiah said, "I am sad because the wall around my city is broken down."

The king said, "You may go and help the people build the wall. Come back when it is finished." Nehemiah was very happy.

When Nehemiah came to the city, he said to all the people, "We can build the wall. We can make it strong again."

Everyone worked together. After many days, the wall was finished. Everyone was glad to see the wall. And Nehemiah was glad God had heard his prayer.

An angel
visits Mary.
Luke 1:26-38

An angel visits Mary.

Luke 1:26-38

God wanted to tell a girl named Mary some good news. When you tell someone good news, you might call on the telephone or write a letter. But God sent an angel to talk to Mary!

One day Mary was alone. She looked up. Standing right there beside her was an angel! Mary had never seen a real angel before. Mary was surprised to see the angel. She was afraid.

The angel said, "Don't be afraid, Mary. God loves you. He has chosen you to be the mother of a very special baby. You will name the baby Jesus. This special baby will be God's own Son!"

Mary was glad to hear this promise. She praised God.

Jesus is born.

Luke 2:1-7

Jesus is born.

Luke 2:1-7

Mary was going to have a baby. An angel had come to tell Mary about this baby. Her baby would be special. He would be God's Son.

When it was time to have her baby, Mary and Joseph had to take a trip. They walked and walked for three days. Finally Mary and Joseph came to Bethlehem. There were so many people that there weren't any rooms left in the inn. There wasn't anywhere else for them to stay.

Finally, Mary and Joseph found a place to stay. It wasn't a nice place. It probably wasn't even a clean place. It was a place for animals to stay! Mary's little baby was born there. Mary wrapped the little baby in some clean cloths and then she laid Him in a manger filled with clean straw. Mary and Joseph named this baby Jesus.

Shepherds come to greet Jesus.
Luke 2:8-20

Shepherds come to greet Jesus.

Luke 2:8-20

The nighttime sky was dark. Out on a hill, some men were sitting together. They were shepherds who were taking care of a flock of sheep. Suddenly, there was a very bright light in the nighttime sky. And right before their eyes they saw an angel! The shepherds were very frightened!

"Do not be afraid," the angel said to them. "I have good news for everyone! Tonight in the city of Bethlehem, Jesus, the Savior, is born! You will find the baby wrapped in cloth and lying in a manger."

Before the shepherds had a chance to say anything, the sky was filled with more and more angels. The angels praised God and said, "Glory to God in the highest!" The shepherds listened as the angels praised God for sending Jesus to be born.

When all the angels had left, the sky became quiet and dark once more. The shepherds said to each other, "Let's go to Bethlehem. We want to see this baby the angel told us about!" They hurried down the hillside and ran along the road to Bethlehem.

When they found the stable, they saw Mary and Joseph. They quietly came near to see the baby. There was baby Jesus lying in a manger, just as the angel had said.

The shepherds were so excited that they told everyone the good news as they went back to their sheep. "Jesus is born! Jesus is born in Bethlehem!" they said. The shepherds thanked God for sending His Son, Jesus.

Jesus escapes to Egypt.
Matthew 2:13-23

Jesus escapes to Egypt.

Matthew 2:13-23

Joseph and Mary and little Jesus were asleep in their house. Joseph had a dream. In the dream, an angel told Joseph to get up quickly and take Mary and little Jesus to Egypt. The angel said that Jesus was in danger because King Herod wanted to kill Him! Joseph got up. He and Mary packed what they needed. They quickly left Bethlehem with Jesus. They traveled all the way to Egypt.

After they left, King Herod sent his soldiers to Bethlehem, the town where Jesus was born. King Herod told his soldiers to kill all the little boys in Bethlehem! It was a horrible thing for the king to do. The king was a very mean man. But Jesus was safe. God had protected Jesus.

Joseph and Mary and baby Jesus stayed in Egypt until the king died. Then an angel came and told Joseph that it was safe for them to go back home. They went to live in Nazareth.

Mary and Joseph look for Jesus.
Luke 2:41-52

Mary and Joseph look for Jesus.

Luke 2:41-52

Crowds of people were on their way home. They had been to Jerusalem for a special celebration. Mary and Joseph were there. They were walking and talking with their friends. They thought Jesus was there in the crowd, too. They thought Jesus was walking and talking with His friends.

Mary and Joseph and their friends walked all day. When it began to get dark, Mary and Joseph started looking for Jesus. *Jesus should be here somewhere* Mary must have thought. Mary and Joseph did not find Jesus. Mary and Joseph were worried. *What happened to Jesus? Did He get hurt? Is He lost?*

They hurried back to Jerusalem. Mary and Joseph looked and looked. Finally they found Jesus. He was sitting in the Temple! Jesus was listening to the teachers. Jesus was asking them questions. The teachers were amazed at Jesus. The teachers were learning from Jesus even though He was just a boy. Mary asked Jesus, "Why are you here? We have been looking for you."

Jesus said, "Why were you looking for me? Didn't you know I had to be in my Father's house?" Jesus went home with Mary and Joseph. Jesus obeyed them.

John the Baptist preaches about the coming Savior.
Matthew 3:1-12; Mark 1:1-8; Luke 3:1-20

John the Baptist preaches about the coming Savior.

Matthew 3:1-12; Mark 1:1-8; Luke 3:1-20

Many people went to the desert. It was hot. People walked a long way. Why did all those people go to the desert? They went to see a preacher: John the Baptist. John the Baptist wore clothes made out of camel's hair. His clothes must have been very itchy!

John the Baptist ate locusts (like big grasshoppers) and wild honey. He didn't have good food like you and I have. John the Baptist didn't care about nice clothes or good-tasting food. John the Baptist cared about telling the people that the Savior of the world was coming.

John told the people to stop doing wrong things and start doing good things. John said, "Share your food with people who don't have any. Don't cheat people or steal from them any more. Be happy with what you have." John said that people needed to be ready because Jesus was coming soon.

John baptizes Jesus.

Matthew 3:13-17; Mark 1:9-11;
Luke 3:21,22; John 1:29-34

John baptizes Jesus.

Matthew 3:13-17; Mark 1:9-11; Luke 3:21,22; John 1:29-34

One day Jesus went to see John the Baptist. John was preaching and baptizing people in the Jordan River. John told people to turn away from doing bad things because the Savior of the world was coming.

Jesus asked John to baptize Him. John knew that Jesus was the Savior of the world. John said, "I am not even good enough to tie your shoes. Why do you ask me to baptize you? You ought to baptize me!" Jesus said that it was right for John to baptize Him.

So John and Jesus waded out into the river. After John baptized Jesus, a dove flew down and landed on Jesus to show that God was with Him. A voice from heaven said, "This is my Son. I am pleased with Him."

When Jesus is tempted, He obeys God's Word.

Matthew 4:1-11; Mark 1:12,13; Luke 4:1-13

When Jesus is tempted, He obeys God's Word.

Matthew 4:1-11; Mark 1:12,13; Luke 4:1-13

One day, Jesus went to a quiet, lonely place in the desert. Jesus was getting ready to do important work for God. Jesus stayed in the desert for 40 days. He did not eat anything the whole time!

At the end of 40 days, God's enemy, Satan, came to see Jesus. Satan wanted Jesus to do something that was wrong.

Satan knew Jesus was very hungry. Satan showed Jesus a stone. "If you want to, you can turn this stone into bread," Satan said. But Jesus told Satan that real life comes from God's Word and is even more important than eating. Jesus knew He shouldn't do what Satan wanted Him to do.

Satan did not give up. Satan took Jesus to the top of a very tall building. "You can prove to everyone you are God's Son," Satan said. "If You jump off this building, angels will come and save You." But Jesus said no. He was not going to do something foolish just to prove God's love for Him.

Satan still did not give up. Satan took Jesus to the top of a very high mountain. He showed Jesus the whole world. "If You worship me instead of God, I will give You this whole world," Satan said to Jesus.

Jesus said, "No! The Bible says people should only worship God." Satan tempted Jesus, but Jesus did what was right. Jesus obeyed God's Word.

Jesus says, "Follow me."

Matthew 4:18-22; Mark 1:16-20; Luke 5:1-11; John 1:40-42

Jesus says, "Follow me."

Matthew 4:18-22; Mark 1:16-20; Luke 5:1-11; John 1:40-42

Peter and Andrew liked to fish. They went fishing every day. Fishing was how they earned money.

One day Jesus came to the Sea of Galilee where they were fishing. Many people wanted to hear Jesus teach. The people kept crowding around Him, trying to get closer. Jesus got into Peter and Andrew's boat. Then Jesus sat down and taught all the people who were crowded on the beach.

When Jesus finished talking to the people, Jesus told Peter to take the boat out into deeper water. Then Jesus told Peter to let down his nets to catch some fish.

When Peter and Andrew let down the nets, they caught so many fish that the nets began to break! Peter and Andrew called to their partners in another boat to come and help them. There were so many fish that when they pulled the nets with the fish into the boats, the boats began to sink. Quickly, the men rowed to shore.

Jesus said, "From now on you will catch people." Jesus meant Peter and Andrew would tell lots of people the good news about Jesus. Peter and Andrew and their partners pulled their boats up on the beach, left everything and followed Jesus.

Jesus teaches in Nazareth.
Luke 4:14-30

Jesus teaches in Nazareth.

Luke 4:14-30

Jesus grew up in the town of Nazareth. One day, when He was a grown up, Jesus went to the synagogue in Nazareth. The synagogue was the place where people came together to learn about and worship God. The men were taking turns reading God's Word aloud.

When it was Jesus' turn, Jesus read God's words written by the prophet Isaiah. The words said that God's Son, the Savior, would come to Earth and make sick people well. The Savior would care for the poor and set people free from the punishment for the wrong things they had done. When Jesus

stopped reading, He said, "Today these words have come true."

The people were amazed! *Did Jesus mean He was the Savior?* Jesus' words made the people angry. They did not believe Jesus was the Savior God had promised to send.

The people became so angry that they took Jesus out of the synagogue. They wanted to hurt Jesus. But Jesus walked away from the angry crowd and went safely on His way to tell people in other places who He was and why He had come to Earth.

Jesus' friends learn to pray.
Matthew 6:5-13; Mark 1:35-37; Luke 11:1-4

Jesus' friends learn to pray.

Matthew 6:5-13; Mark 1:35-37; Luke 11:1-4

One evening, Jesus stayed at a house with some of His friends. When morning came, Jesus' friends heard the sound of voices outside the house. Many people had come to see Jesus.

Jesus' friends looked for Jesus. They looked inside and outside the house for Him. But they did not find Jesus anywhere! So they walked down the road to look for Him. When Jesus' friends came to a quiet place, they saw Jesus. He was all alone, praying. He was talking to God, His Father in heaven.

Jesus' friends knew that Jesus liked to pray. Many times His friends had seen Jesus praying. And now they saw that Jesus would even get up early in the morning to pray!

Soon after, Jesus' friends asked Him to teach them to pray. Jesus told them to talk to God just as they would talk to a father who loves them very

much. Jesus said to ask God the Father for what they needed each day. Jesus said to ask God to forgive them for the wrong things they did, and to forgive other people for wrong things they did to them, too. Jesus also said to ask God to help them do right things.

"When you pray," Jesus said, "pray like this:

'Our Father who is in heaven, holy is Your name.

We want You to be our King.

Give us what we need today.

Forgive the wrong things we do.

We forgive everyone who has done wrong to us.

Please protect us. Help us to do right.

You are the King. You can do anything.

Amen.'"

Jesus talks about the birds and the flowers.
Matthew 6:25-34

Jesus talks about the birds and the flowers.

Matthew 6:25-34

Jesus was talking to people on a hillside. There were old people and young people, parents and children and grandparents. Jesus told the people not to worry. He said they didn't need to worry about having enough to eat or drink. They didn't need to worry about what clothes they should wear.

Jesus pointed to the sky. Birds were flying. Jesus said, "Look at the birds! They don't plant seeds to grow crops. They don't gather up food like farmers. But God makes sure they have enough food to eat. God loves them and takes care of them. Don't you think you are more important to God than the birds? Of course you are! So don't worry. Ask God for help. He will take care of you."

The people looked up at the birds and thought about what Jesus said. They were thankful God would care for them.

Then Jesus pointed at some flowers. He talked about how beautiful they were. He told the people that flowers don't make their own clothes, but their clothes were more beautiful than anything a king would wear. "If God takes care of the flowers that well," Jesus asked, "don't you think He would certainly take care of you, too?"

"Instead of worrying about food or clothes," Jesus said, "ask God what He wants you to do. When you obey God and do what is right, God will give you what you need. Don't worry about tomorrow. God will take care of you today and tomorrow!"

All the people were glad to hear that God loved them. They were glad to know they could ask God for help and He would take care of them.

Jesus teaches about the wise and foolish men.
Matthew 7:24-29

Jesus teaches about the wise and foolish men.

Matthew 7:24-29

One day Jesus told a story about building a house. He said, "A wise man built his house on a strong rock. Then the rain came, the river rose, and the winds blew! But the house did not fall down. It was built on strong rock. This wise man is like a person who listens to Me and obeys My words."

"But," said Jesus, "a foolish man built his house on the sand. When the rain and winds came, the house on the sand fell down. It wasn't built on something strong. A person who hears My words but won't follow them is like this foolish man."

Jesus told this story about the wise and foolish men to help people learn how important it is to obey Jesus' words. Jesus' words are true and help people know the best way to live.

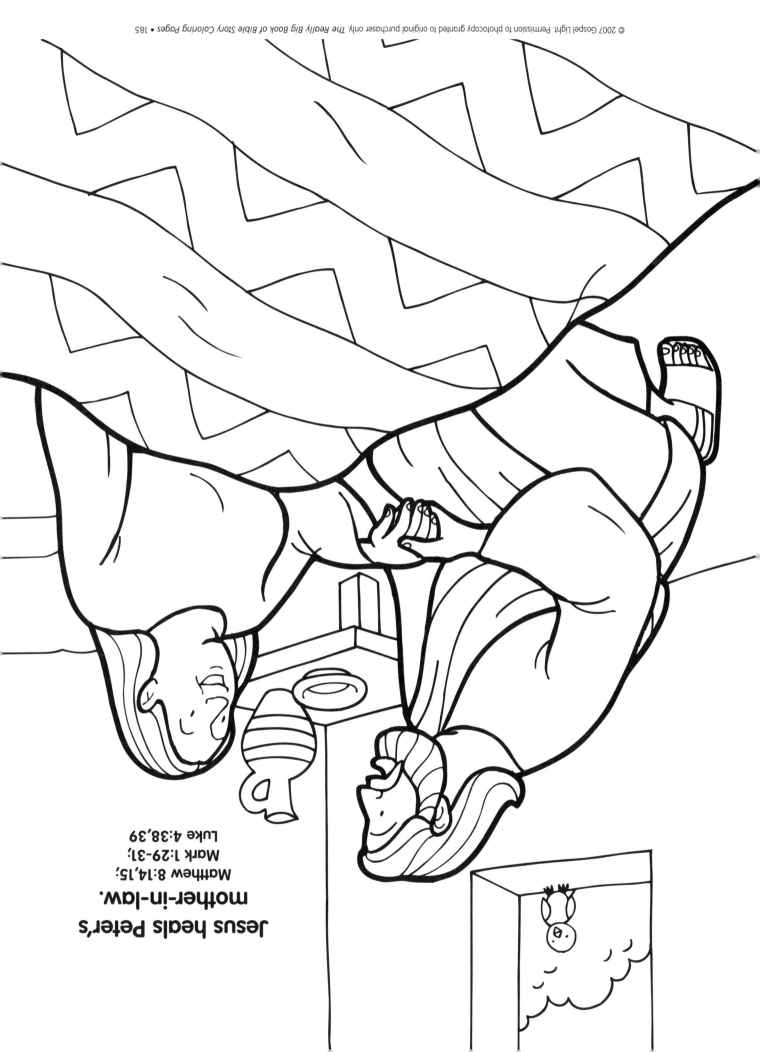

Jesus heals Peter's mother-in-law.
Matthew 8:14,15;
Mark 1:29-31;
Luke 4:38,39

Jesus heals Peter's mother-in-law.

Matthew 8:14,15; Mark 1:29-31; Luke 4:38,39

Peter's wife's mother was sick. She lay in bed. Her head was hot. Her family felt afraid. They wanted her to get well.

Jesus and His friends went to Peter's house. Peter's family asked Jesus to help her get well. Jesus bent down and touched her hand. Right away she was well! She got up and helped to serve food to Jesus and His friends.

The Pharisees question Jesus.
Matthew 12:1-14; Mark 2:23—3:6; Luke 6:1-11

The Pharisees question Jesus.

Matthew 12:1-14; Mark 2:23—3:6; Luke 6:1-11

When Jesus lived on Earth, the Pharisees were the religious leaders. They tried to be sure that everyone followed God's rules. They even made up more rules of their own. They said that obeying these rules was the only way to show love for God. But Jesus said that what God most wanted was for people to love God and love each other.

One of the Pharisees' rules was that a person could not do any work on the seventh day of the week. The seventh day was called the Sabbath. One Sabbath, Jesus and his friends were walking along a road where grain was growing. Jesus' friends picked some grain and ate it.

The Pharisees saw Jesus' friends pick the grain! The Pharisees thought that picking grain was

work. They asked Jesus why He didn't stop His friends from picking grain. Jesus reminded the Pharisees that God was not angry with people who worked to get food when they were hungry.

Later on the Sabbath, Jesus saw a man whose hand was crippled. The Pharisees thought that Jesus should not help the man. Making his hand well was work! But Jesus knew how important it was to show love and help someone in need. Jesus made the crippled man's hand well! The man must have been glad and thankful!

Jesus wanted everyone to know that caring for people's needs was one of the best ways to show love for God.

Jesus talks to Nicodemus about God's love.
John 3:1-21

Jesus talks to Nicodemus about God's love.

John 3:1-21

The Pharisees were people who thought they knew all about God. Most of the Pharisees didn't like Jesus. They were afraid people wouldn't pay any attention to them if Jesus kept teaching. Most of the Pharisees wanted to make Jesus stop teaching and healing people.

Nicodemus was a Pharisee. But Nicodemus wanted to learn more about Jesus. He went to see Jesus at night when no one else was around.

Jesus told Nicodemus that God loved everyone in the world so much that God sent His Son Jesus to die on the cross. Because of that, everyone who believes in Jesus can have eternal life with Jesus. Nicodemus didn't understand everything that Jesus said. Jesus explained that when people believe in Jesus, they are forgiven for the wrong things they do.

Jesus talks to a
Samaritan woman.
John 4:1-42

Jesus talks to a Samaritan woman.

John 4:1-42

Jesus and His friends walked to the country of Samaria. It was a long walk. Jesus was tired, so He sat down by a well to rest. Jesus' friends went into town to find some food to eat.

While Jesus' friends were gone, a woman came to the well to get some water. It was very hot outside. The sun was very bright. The woman brought a big jar to fill with water. It must have been hard work to carry the heavy jar.

"May I have a drink?" Jesus asked. The woman was surprised! Men never talked to women in public places back then. Jesus told the woman some secrets she had. Jesus showed her that He cared about her. Jesus told her He was the Messiah—the Savior God promised to send. The woman went back to the town to tell others about Jesus. She brought many people back to see Jesus so they could hear Him, too.

The centurion's servant is made well.

Luke 7:1-10

The centurion's servant is made well.

Luke 7:1-10

There was a man who was a leader in the Roman army. He was a centurion. People living in Israel did not like the Roman army. But this centurion was different. He helped the Jewish leaders build a place to worship God.

One day this centurion's servant became very sick. The centurion could not do anything to help the servant get better. Then the centurion remembered hearing about Jesus, who made sick people well. The centurion asked his Jewish friends to talk to Jesus and ask Him to help the sick servant.

The Jewish men went to talk to Jesus. They told Him about the centurion and the sick servant. Jesus said He would go with them to help the servant. So they hurried toward the centurion's house. But before they got to the house, they met some of the centurion's friends. They had a

message for Jesus.

"The centurion asked us to tell Jesus this: 'You don't need to come to my house. Just give the order to make my servant well. I know You will make him well.'"

When Jesus heard these words, He was amazed! He turned to the people with Him. He said, "I haven't seen this much faith before! Go! The servant will be made well."

The friends hurried back to the house. When they got there, they found the sick servant was now completely well! The centurion believed Jesus could help his servant, and Jesus did!

Jesus stops a funeral.
Luke 7:11-17

Jesus stops a funeral.

Luke 7:11-17

Jesus and his friends were walking on a road near a town. They met a group of people who were sad and crying. The people were carrying a dead boy out of the town to bury him.

One woman was very, very sad. The dead boy was her only son! Her husband had already died. Now she was the only one left in her family. Jesus looked at this woman. He felt sorry for her and told her not to cry.

Then Jesus said, "Young man, get up!" And the dead boy sat up! He was alive again! Everyone who was watching was completely amazed. They praised God because they had seen this boy come back to life.

The mother must have been glad and thankful. Her son was alive again! The news about Jesus' love and power spread everywhere!

Jesus calms a storm.
Matthew 8:23-27; Mark 4:35-41;
Luke 8:22-25

Jesus calms a storm.
Matthew 8:23-27; Mark 4:35-41; Luke 8:22-25

One night Jesus and His friends were sailing across the lake in their boat. Jesus was very tired. He lay down in the back of the boat. Soon He was asleep.

Suddenly, the wind began to blow. The wind blew harder and harder. The little waves got bigger and bigger. The big waves hit hard against the little boat. Water splashed into the boat. The boat was filling with water.

Jesus' friends were afraid. But Jesus slept quietly through the storm.

"Jesus! Help us!" shouted a friend. "Don't you care that our boat is sinking?"

Jesus woke up. Jesus stood up and said, "Quiet! Be still!" And just like that, the wind stopped blowing. The big waves stopped splashing.

"Why were you so afraid?" Jesus asked His friends. "Don't you know that I will take care of you?"

Jesus' friends were amazed that the winds and the waves had obeyed Jesus.

Jesus heals a paralyzed man.
Matthew 9:2-8; Mark 2:1-12; Luke 5:17-26

Jesus heals a paralyzed man.

Matthew 9:2-8; Mark 2:1-12; Luke 5:17-26

Many people came to hear Jesus teach. They crowded into the house. They even stood around the outside of the house. Some men came carrying their friend on a mat. Their friend couldn't move. He just had to lie on his mat.

The men wanted Jesus to help their friend, but they couldn't get through the crowd to bring their friend to Jesus. The men carried their friend up some stairs to the flat roof of the house. They dug a hole in the roof right over where Jesus was standing. They put ropes on their friend's mat. They carefully lowered the mat down in front of Jesus.

Jesus saw that the men believed in Him. Jesus told the man on the mat that his sins were forgiven. Then Jesus told him to get up. The man got up. He could walk! The crowd was amazed. They praised God!

A woman touches Jesus and is healed.
Matthew 9:20-22; Mark 5:25-34; Luke 8:43-48

A woman touches Jesus and is healed.

Matthew 9:20-22; Mark 5:25-34; Luke 8:43-48

There were many people all around Jesus. Everyone wanted to be close to Jesus. Everyone wanted to hear what He said. Everyone wanted to see what He did. Suddenly, Jesus asked, "Who touched me?"

Jesus' friends looked around. "There are many people here. We're all bumping into each other," they said.

"No," Jesus replied. "Someone touched me. I know that power has gone out from me."

A woman came and bowed before Jesus. "I touched you because I wanted to be healed. I have been sick for many years. As soon as I touched you, I could tell that I wasn't sick anymore!"

Jesus smiled and said, "Your faith has healed you. Go in peace."

Jesus sends out 12 helpers.
Matthew 10:1-11

Jesus sends out 12 helpers.

Matthew 10:1-11

Many people followed Jesus wherever He went. They listened to Him teach about God. Twelve of these people were Jesus' special helpers: Simon (called Peter) and his brother Andrew, James son of Zebedee and his brother John, Philip, Bartholomew, Thomas, Matthew, James son of Alphaeus, Thaddaeus, Simon and Judas Iscariot.

Jesus taught these 12 men about God. He told them how to make sick people well. Then Jesus sent them to tell more people about Jesus and to show God's power by helping others.

Jesus told His helpers to travel in pairs. He told them they didn't need to take very much with them. They didn't need a bag with extra clothes or shoes, or even money. Instead, Jesus' helpers could depend on God to care for them. In each town they visited, they would find someone who would let them stay at his or her home.

Jesus' helpers did just what Jesus told them to do. They traveled to many towns. They told many people about God.

Jesus tells the parable of the sower.
Mark 4:1-20

Jesus tells the parable of the sower.

Mark 4:1-20

One day, Jesus told a crowd this story: "A farmer went out to his field to plant some seeds. The farmer tossed seeds onto the ground. Some seeds fell on the hard dirt. The birds ate these seeds.

"Other seeds fell on rocky ground. The plants grew for a little while. But there wasn't enough water, and the plants soon died. Other seeds fell near thorny weeds. The weeds grew faster and stronger than the plants. The plants couldn't grow! These plants died, too."

Finally Jesus said that some of the seed fell on good soil. Those seeds grew and became a huge good crop. Jesus' friends wondered, *What does this story mean?*

Jesus said, "The seeds are like God's Word. People who hear God's Word but never believe it are

like the hard dirt where birds ate the seeds. Some people are glad to hear the Word of God. They believe it, but later it's too hard to do what God wants. They stop believing God's Word. They are like the rocky soil."

One of the friends asked, "What kind of people are like the thorny soil?"

Jesus said, "Some people hear and believe God's Word. They begin to grow, but then their worries keep them from growing. Soon they forget about God's Word.

"The good soil is like people who hear and believe God's Word. They are glad to always love and obey God."

Jesus told this story to teach His helpers to obey God's Word.

Jesus uses a boy's lunch to feed 5,000 people.

Matthew 14:13-21; Mark 6:30-44; Luke 9:10-17; John 6:1-15

Jesus uses a boy's lunch to feed 5,000 people.

Matthew 14:13-21; Mark 6:30-44; Luke 9:10-17; John 6:1-15

Many people followed Jesus. They listened to Him talk all day long. They didn't have any food to eat and it was getting late. The people were hungry. They were a long way from a town with food.

Jesus told His friends to give the people something to eat. Jesus' friends didn't have enough food for all the people. Only one little boy had some food. It was just enough for one person to have lunch, but the little boy wanted to share his food.

Jesus told the people to sit down. Jesus took the boy's lunch and prayed. Then Jesus broke off pieces of bread and fish. His friends gave the food to the people. There was more than enough for everyone to eat. It was a miracle—something only God could do. One little boy's lunch became enough food for everyone to eat!

Jesus walks on the water and helps His friends.

Matthew 14:22-33; Mark 6:45-52; John 6:16-21

Jesus walks on the water and helps His friends.

Matthew 14:22-33; Mark 6:45-52; John 6:16-21

Jesus' friends were in a boat on the Sea of Galilee. The waves were coming over the side of the boat. The waves were very strong. Jesus' friends worked hard to row the boat.

Suddenly, Jesus' friends saw something that terrified them! They saw a man walking on the water. Jesus' friends knew that people couldn't walk on water. They thought they were seeing a ghost!

Jesus called out to them. "Don't be afraid," He said. "It's Me!" When Peter realized it was Jesus walking on the water, Peter wanted to walk out to Him. Jesus told Peter to come. Peter started to walk on the water to Jesus. When Peter looked at the waves, he was afraid and started to sink. Jesus took Peter by the hand and pulled him up. They got into the boat, and at once the sea was still.

Jesus heals
a man who
couldn't
hear or talk.
Mark 7:31-37

Jesus heals a man who couldn't hear or talk.

Mark 7:31-37

Some people brought to Jesus a man who couldn't hear or talk. "Please make this man well," they said.

Jesus walked a little way away with the man. Jesus didn't want everyone in the crowd that was following Him to listen when He talked to the man.

Jesus put His fingers into the man's ears. Then Jesus spit and touched the man's tongue. Jesus looked up to heaven. He said, "Be opened!" As soon as Jesus said this, the man could hear and he could talk plainly.

Jesus told the man and his friends not to tell others what had happened, but they were so amazed that they just kept on talking about the wonderful thing Jesus did.

Jesus' friends hear that Jesus is God's Son.

Matthew 17:1-13; Luke 9:28-36

Jesus' friends hear that Jesus is God's Son.

Matthew 17:1-13; Luke 9:28-36

One day Jesus asked Peter, James and John to go with Him to a place high on a mountain. When they had climbed up to where Jesus wanted them to go, they began to pray together. But as Jesus prayed, His face and clothes became brighter and brighter. Jesus' face was as bright as the sun. His clothes were as white as the light.

Peter, James and John were very surprised. Suddenly, two other men appeared and talked to Jesus. The three friends saw that these men were Moses and Elijah. Moses and Elijah were great prophets. Moses and Elijah had lived a long time ago.

Peter told Jesus that he would build three little shelters for Moses, Elijah and Jesus. But as Peter was speaking, a bright cloud shone all around them. They could hardly see! Then they heard God's voice. God said, "This is My Son, whom I love. Listen to Him!"

After hearing these words, Peter, James and John were afraid! They fell down on the ground and covered their faces with their hands. But then the three friends heard Jesus' quiet voice telling them not to be afraid. Peter, James and John saw that Moses and Elijah were gone. The bright light was not shining anymore. Jesus and His friends walked down the mountain. Peter, James and John must have remembered this special day for a long time!

Jesus tells about a big party.
Luke 14:1,15-24

Jesus tells about a big party.

Luke 14:1,15-24

Jesus was eating dinner with a group of people. As they ate, Jesus told a story to help these people understand something very important about God's family.

"A man planned to have a big party at his house. There would be lots of good food and music. When everything was ready, the man sent his servant to tell the guests that it was time to come. But the guests made excuses about why they could not come to the party!

"One guest said he was too busy looking at his new oxen. Another guest said he needed to see some land he had just bought. And another man said he was too busy with his new wife.

"The man giving the party heard all these excuses, but he still wanted to have the party! He told his servant to bring all of the poor, the blind, the crippled and the lame people to his feast.

"The servant ran through the streets. He asked everyone he saw who was poor, blind, crippled or lame to come to the party. And they all came! Some people carried anyone who couldn't walk. Other people led those who couldn't see. Finally the whole banquet hall was filled up. They ate delicious food and heard lovely music. Everybody had a wonderful time!"

Jesus told this story to remind us that no one should make an excuse when God invites us to be a part of His family. God loves all people. He doesn't want anyone to miss a chance to know Him.

Jesus tells about a patient father.

Luke 15:11-32

Jesus tells about a patient father.

Luke 15:11-32

Jesus told a story about a man and his two sons. The younger son asked his father for the money that he would one day inherit. The father gave the son what the son wanted.

Soon after that, the younger son took all his money and went to another country. He spent all his money on parties and buying things for his friends. After his money was gone there was a famine. There was no food for him to eat! None of his friends would help him. The only work he could find was feeding pigs. He was so hungry that he wanted to eat the food the pigs were eating!

Finally the son realized what he should do. He decided to go back home and ask to be hired as one of his father's servants. When the son was still far away, his father saw him. His father ran to him and threw his arms around him.

The son said, "Father, I was wrong. I'm not good enough to be called your son." But the father called to his servants. "Bring some new clothes for my son," he said. "Get ready for a party! My son has come home!"

Only one man says thank-you to Jesus.
Luke 17:11-19

Only one man says thank-you to Jesus.

Luke 17:11-19

Jesus and His friends were walking. As they came near a village, Some men saw Jesus. These ten men had a disease called leprosy. The ten men didn't run to Jesus because people who had leprosy had to stay away from everyone! That was the law. So the men with leprosy called out to Jesus. They said, "Jesus, have pity on us!"

When Jesus saw and heard the men, He told them to go and show themselves to the priests. As the ten men walked to the priests, they saw that they were cured. None of them had leprosy anymore!

One of the ten men turned around and ran back to Jesus. He started to praise God in a loud voice. Other people must have heard him. Other people must have been excited to see him healthy instead of sick. The man thanked Jesus for healing him.

Jesus said, "Didn't I heal ten men? Where are the other nine?" Then Jesus said to the man who came back, "Get up and go. Your faith has made you well." The healed man was very happy!

Jesus tells the story of the forgiving king.
Matthew 18:21-35

© 2007 Gospel Light. Permission to photocopy granted to original purchaser only. *The Really Big Book of Bible Story Coloring Pages* • 221

Jesus tells the story of the forgiving king.

Matthew 18:21-35

One day, Peter asked Jesus, "Lord, how many times should I forgive a person who has been unkind to me?" Jesus answered Peter by telling him a story.

"Once there was a man who worked for a king. This man had asked the king for lots and lots of money. The man promised to pay it all back. One day the king told this man, 'Pay back all the money you borrowed from me. Pay me right now!' But this man did not have the money. He could not pay the king.

"The king called his servants and said, 'Sell everything this man has. I will take that money to pay what he owes me!'

"The man got down on his knees in front of the king. 'No! No!' he cried. 'Please wait! I promise to pay you back all the money I owe you!'

"The king felt sorry for the man. He said, 'Get up. I forgive you. You do not have to pay back any of the money you borrowed.'

"The man was very happy! On his way home from talking to the king, he saw a friend of his. This friend had borrowed a little money from him. The man grabbed his friend. He shouted, 'Give me back all my money!'

"The friend got down on his knees. He begged, 'Please wait. I promise to pay you back.' But the man would not forgive his friend. He had his friend put in jail!

"When the king heard about the unkind way that this man had treated his friend, the king called the man to come to him. 'You are a mean man!' the king said. 'I forgave you. I did not make you pay back ANY of the money you owed me! But you did not forgive your friend. You will be punished for your unkindness.' So the king had the man put into jail."

When Jesus finished the story, He said, "God wants you to ALWAYS forgive other people, even when they have been unkind to you."

Jesus tells the story of the lost sheep.
Matthew 18:10-14; Luke 15:3-7

Jesus tells the story of the lost sheep.

Matthew 18:10-14; Luke 15:3-7

Jesus told a story about a shepherd who had 100 sheep.

"This shepherd loved his sheep and took good care of them. The shepherd carried a long stick called a staff. If a sheep would start to walk too far away, the shepherd tapped the sheep with his staff, so it would come back. Sometimes the shepherd used the staff to help a sheep get up after it had fallen.

"Every day, the shepherd counted his sheep as he let them out of the fold. He counted all 100 sheep and made sure they were there. Then he led his sheep out to the hillsides so that they could eat green grass. The sheep drank cool water, too. The shepherd made sure the sheep had enough to eat and drink.

"One day, the shepherd counted his sheep, but he only counted 99! One of the sheep was gone! The shepherd hurried off to find his lost sheep. He looked all over! Then the shepherd heard a little 'Baaa!' He heard it again and looked some more. 'BAAAA!' Then he saw the lost sheep.

"The shepherd reached down and gently lifted the sheep up from where it was stuck. The shepherd laid the sheep across his shoulders. He carried the sheep back to where the other sheep were. The good shepherd was very glad he had found his lost sheep! And the sheep was glad to be back with the good shepherd who always loved and cared for it.

"God loves us like that," Jesus said. "He is glad when we accept His love and obey Him."

Jesus tells about the good shepherd.
John 10:7-18

Jesus tells about the good shepherd.

John 10:7-18

Jesus told about a shepherd who took good care of his sheep. Each day he took them to a good place to eat green plants. He found cool water for them to drink. He scared away all the wolves that tried to sneak up on the sheep while they were eating. He knew the name of each sheep. The sheep knew the shepherd's voice, too. They would not come when a stranger called them.

When nighttime came, the shepherd led his sheep to a sheepfold made of rock walls. There was only one doorway. The shepherd counted his sheep as they walked in. When each sheep was inside, the shepherd would lie down to sleep right across the doorway! That way, no robber or wolf could get

into the fold and hurt the sheep. The shepherd protected his sheep.

Jesus told the people listening to the story that they were like sheep! And Jesus said He was like the good shepherd.

Jesus said, "I am the One who protects the sheep. My sheep will be safe because I am their shepherd. I have come so that My sheep might have the best kind of life there is!"

"I am the Good Shepherd," Jesus said. "I give My own life for My sheep." Jesus meant that He loves people so much that He was going to die on the cross to pay for the wrong things we do.

Jesus tells about a good Samaritan.

Luke 10:25-37

Jesus tells about a good Samaritan.
Luke 10:25-37

Jesus told this story: A man was going from Jerusalem to Jericho, when he got hurt by some robbers. The robbers took everything the man had and beat him up. Then they went away, leaving him hurt and almost dead.

A priest happened to be walking down the same road. When he saw the man, he passed by on the other side of the road. A Levite (a helper in the Temple) also walked by and saw the hurt man. The Levite didn't help the man either. But then, a Samaritan man came to where the man was. The Samaritan saw that the man was Jewish. He knew that Jews and Samaritans did not like each other. But the Samaritan stopped to help. He bandaged the hurt man's sores and put the man on his own donkey. The Samaritan took him to an inn. He even paid the innkeeper to take care of the hurt man!

Jesus asked, "Who was a neighbor to the man who got hurt?" The one who was a neighbor was the one who helped the hurt man. Jesus wants everyone to help others the same way.

Jesus loves the children.
Matthew 19:13-15; Mark 10:13-16; Luke 18:15-17

Jesus loves the children.

Matthew 19:13-15; Mark 10:13-16; Luke 18:15-17

One day Jesus was teaching His friends and other people about God. They were listening carefully to what Jesus was saying. Just then, a group of people came to see Jesus.

Jesus and His friends looked at these people and saw that it was children and their parents. The children and their mothers and fathers were so excited to see Jesus.

But when they came near to Jesus, His friends thought that Jesus was too busy to talk to the children. Jesus' friends said, "Don't bring those children here!" The children and their parents were sad to hear those words. They started to walk away.

But wait! Jesus said, "Let the children come to Me! I want to see them!" Jesus was not too busy to see the children! Jesus loved them!

Right away, the children ran to Jesus. They crowded close to Him. Some even climbed up on His lap. Jesus put His arms around them. What a happy day! The children knew Jesus loved them!

Jesus helps a blind man see.
John 9:1-41

Jesus helps a blind man see.

John 9:1-41

One day Jesus saw a man who had been blind his whole life. The man had never seen grass or the sky or his mom's face. Jesus took some dirt, spit in it and made some mud. Then Jesus put the mud on the man's eyes. Jesus told the man to wash his eyes in a pool of water. The man went and washed his eyes just like Jesus said. Then the man could see!

When the man got home, many people were amazed. Some people asked, "Isn't this the same man who used to sit and beg?"

Others said, "No, he only looks like the blind man."

But the man born blind said, "I am the one. Jesus made some mud and put it on my eyes. Then Jesus told me to go and wash my eyes in a pool of water. So I did and now I can see."

A rich man asks Jesus a question.
Matthew 19:16-26; Mark 10:17-27

A rich man asks Jesus a question.

Matthew 19:16-26; Mark 10:17-27

All day long Jesus had been busy teaching people about God. Now Jesus was leaving town. A very rich young man ran up to Jesus. He knelt down in front of Him. "Teacher," asked the rich man, "what should I do so that I can live forever?"

Jesus said, "If you want to have life that lasts forever, do all the things God has said to do." The young man asked what those things were.

"You know what God has said to do," Jesus answered. "Do not kill anyone. Do not take anything that doesn't belong to you. Do not tell lies. Love and obey your father and mother. Love others the same way you love yourself."

The rich man said he had obeyed all of these things since he was a little boy. He had done a

lot of right things! Jesus loved the young man. But Jesus knew the man loved his money more than he loved God. So Jesus said, "There is one thing more you need to do. Sell everything you have. Give the money to poor people. Then come and follow Me."

That rich young man had a lot that he could sell! But he didn't want to share any of it. He wanted to keep it all! The rich man stood up, turned around and sadly walked away.

Jesus told His friends, "It is very hard for people who love money to love and obey God." Jesus' friends were surprised! They wondered then who could have life that lasts forever. Jesus said that only God could help them.

Jesus tells the story of the workers.
Matthew 20:1-16

Jesus tells the story of the workers.

Matthew 20:1-16

Jesus told a story to explain God's generous love.

"Early one morning a farmer hired some workers to help gather his big crop of grapes. The farmer told the men how much he would pay them for a day's work. After the men had worked for a few hours, the farmer hired more workers. Those men joined the others picking grapes.

"About noon, the farmer hired even more workers! But there were so many grapes to be picked that the farmer hired more workers two more times!

"When the day was over, the farmer told his helper to gather all the workers and pay them. He told his helper to pay the workers hired last and then end with the men hired first.

"The helper paid each worker the same amount of money. The workers who had only worked for one hour were paid the same as the men who had worked all day! The first workers complained, 'We worked all day in the hot sun for you. But you paid us the same that you paid the men who worked only an hour!'

"The farmer said that he paid each worker exactly what he had promised. The farmer was being very generous to pay all the men the same amount."

Jesus told this story so that we would know that God is like the generous farmer. No matter if we accept God's love when we're little or when we're old, God generously gives the free gift of eternal life to anyone who believes in Jesus!

A woman shows love to Jesus.

Matthew 26:6-13; Mark 14:3-9; John 12:2-8

A woman shows love to Jesus.

Matthew 26:6-13; Mark 14:3-9; John 12:2-8

Jesus and some of His friends were having dinner at Simon's house. A woman came into the room holding a jar of very expensive perfume. The woman opened the jar and poured the perfume on Jesus' head and feet. The wonderful smell of the perfume filled the house.

Some of Jesus' friends were not happy. "Why did she waste this expensive perfume?" they said. "She could have sold it and given the money to the poor."

Jesus said, "Don't bother her. She has done a beautiful thing. You can always give to the poor, but I won't always be here like this." Jesus was glad the woman had shown how much she loved Him.

Zacchaeus climbs
a tree to see Jesus.
Luke 19:1-9

Zacchaeus climbs a tree to see Jesus.

Luke 19:1-9

Many people followed Jesus. They wanted to see what He did and hear what He said. There were so many people that Zacchaeus couldn't see. He stood on his tiptoes, but he still couldn't see. He jumped up and down, but the other people were too tall. He asked taller people to move over, but they ignored him. Zacchaeus was too short. And nobody would help him because Zacchaeus had cheated them all out of a lot of money.

Finally, Zacchaeus ran ahead of the crowd. Zacchaeus found a tree that he knew Jesus would pass by. Zacchaeus climbed the tree and waited.

The crowd came closer. Now Zacchaeus could see Jesus! Jesus was coming toward the tree! Jesus stopped under the tree. Jesus looked up at Zacchaeus and said, "Zacchaeus, come down. I must stay at your house today." Zacchaeus was excited!

Zacchaeus climbed down the tree and hurried home with Jesus. Zacchaeus wanted to do what was right. He gave half of everything he had to the poor. He promised to give back four times anything he had stolen. Zacchaeus was glad Jesus loved him.

Jesus brings Lazarus
back to life.
John 11:1-44

Jesus brings Lazarus back to life.

John 11:1-44

Some men ran to Jesus. "Your friend, Lazarus, is very sick. Please come and heal him." Jesus wanted to help Lazarus. But instead of going right away to see Lazarus, Jesus waited. Then Jesus told His friends, "Let's go see Lazarus."

Jesus and His friends walked a long way. They finally got to the place where Lazarus lived. Lazarus's sister Martha went out to meet Jesus.

"Oh, Jesus," she said, "if you had been here my brother would not have died!" Martha, her sister Mary and many other people were so sad because Lazarus had died. Many of them were crying. Jesus saw all the sad people and He started to cry too.

Jesus and all the people went to the tomb where they put Lazarus's body. Jesus said, "Take away the stone."

Jesus prayed. Then Jesus said, "Lazarus, come out!" Lazarus came out of the tomb. Lazarus wasn't dead anymore! He was alive because Jesus raised him from the dead!

Jesus enters Jerusalem.

Matthew 21:1-11; Luke 19:29-44; John 12:12-19

Jesus enters Jerusalem.

Matthew 21:1-11; Luke 19:29-44; John 12:12-19

It was a wonderful day! Crowds of people were on their way to the Temple in Jerusalem. Jesus was going to the Temple, too. But first, Jesus asked two of His friends to bring Him a donkey. His friends found the donkey just where Jesus told them to go. After they brought the donkey to Jesus, they laid their coats over its back for Jesus to sit on as He rode into the city.

The people in the crowd heard that Jesus was coming. Some people cut branches from trees to welcome Jesus. They laid the branches on the road. Other people took off their coats and laid them on the road. People welcomed Jesus the way they would welcome a king. They sang to Jesus, "Hosanna! Hosanna! God bless the One who comes in the name of the Lord!" ("Hosanna" means "Save us!")

The people in Jerusalem heard the singing. They saw the great big crowd coming. Even more people ran to see Jesus and shout "Hosanna! Jesus rode the little donkey up to the Temple. Jesus got off of the donkey and went into the Temple. The children danced around Him, singing and shouting "Hosanna!" What an exciting day it was!

Jesus clears the Temple.
Matthew 21:12-16; Mark 11:12-19; Luke 19:45-48

Jesus clears the Temple.

Matthew 21:12-16; Mark 11:12-19; Luke 19:45-48

Jesus went to the Temple. The Temple was a special place for talking to God and learning about Him. But there were people in the Temple who were making noise selling things.

"Doves for sale!" someone shouted.

"Buy your lambs over here!" Someone else called. They were charging too much and cheating the people. The sellers were so loud that people who wanted to pray couldn't. No one could talk to God or learn about Him when people were yelling like that.

When Jesus saw this, He was angry. Jesus forced the sellers to leave the Temple. Then sick people came to Jesus. Jesus healed them and talked to the people about God.

Jesus tells the parable of the talents.
Matthew 25:14-30; Luke 19:12-27

Jesus tells the parable of the talents.

Matthew 25:14-30; Luke 19:12-27

One day Jesus told about a rich man who had three servants. This man had to go on a long trip. While he was gone, he wanted his servants to make more money for him.

The man gave the first servant five talents. (A talent was a large amount of money.) He gave the second servant two talents, and he gave the third servant one talent. Then he left on his trip.

The servant with five talents went right to work. He used the money to make five more talents! The servant who had gotten two talents also got right to work. He may have bought and sold animals or planted food to sell. Whatever he did, he ended up with four talents—twice what the rich man had given him.

But the last servant was afraid that the money would get lost or stolen. So he dug a hole in the ground and buried the money!

The rich man came back from his trip. He called together his servants to see what they had done with their money. The first servant told that he had gotten five more talents. The second servant showed that he had gotten two more talents. The man was very pleased with their hard work. He said he would give them even more to take care of.

Then the last servant said he had buried the talent in the ground. The rich man was angry! He said he wanted his money to be used, not hidden away.

Jesus told about the rich man to help us know that God wants us to use what He gives us to do good things.

A poor woman
gives all she has.
Mark 12:41-44; Luke 21:1-4

A poor woman gives all she has.
Mark 12:41-44; Luke 21:1-4

Jesus and His friends were sitting by the Temple. Many people came by to give money to God at the Temple. They walked up to a big metal box and dropped their money inside. CLANG! CLANG! The money made lots of noise. Some rich people put in lots of money. The money banged and clanged and everyone looked at the rich people.

Then a poor woman went to the box. She only had two tiny coins. She very quietly dropped her tiny coins into the box. Her money didn't make any noise. No one turned and looked. But Jesus saw what she did. "This woman has given more than any of the rich people," Jesus told His friends. "The others just gave some of their money. She gave all her money."

Jesus washes His friends' feet.

John 13:1-17

Jesus washes His friends' feet.

John 13:1-17

Jesus and His friends were getting ready to have a special dinner together. They spent the day talking and walking. The roads were hot and dusty.

When Jesus and His friends came to the house for a special dinner, their feet were dirty. They needed to be washed! But no one wanted to wash other people's feet. That was a job for a servant!

Jesus waited until the food was on the table. Then Jesus got up and wrapped a towel around His waist. Jesus poured water into a large bowl and began to wash His friends' feet.

Peter felt embarrassed. Peter knew that he should have offered to wash Jesus' feet. But Jesus told Peter that he needed Jesus to wash his feet for him.

"Follow my example," Jesus said. He wanted them to help each other.

Jesus eats a last meal with His friends.

Matthew 26:17-30; Mark 14:12-26; Luke 22:7-20; John 13:1-17

Jesus eats a last meal with His friends.

Matthew 26:17-30; Mark 14:12-26; Luke 22:7-20; John 13:1-17

All over Jerusalem, people were getting ready to eat the Passover dinner. This special meal helped them remember when God helped the Israelites escape from Egypt. Jesus and His friends were going to eat this special meal, too.

When Jesus and his friends came into the house where they would eat, their feet were dirty and dusty. Jesus poured water into a bowl. He began to wash His friends' feet. Jesus' friends thought only servants should do this job! But Jesus explained that washing their feet meant that Jesus loved His friends. And He told them to follow His example and show love to others.

As they ate together, Jesus told them that He would die soon but that His death was part of

God's plan. It was going to happen just the way God said it would happen.

As they ate together, Jesus broke some of the bread into pieces and gave it to His friends. Jesus said the bread was like His body. His body would be broken for them when He died on the cross. Then Jesus passed around the cup of wine. He said they should drink it and remember that He would shed His blood for many people on the cross.

Jesus told His friends how much He loved them. He promised to send the Holy Spirit to help them. The friends listened carefully. They wanted to remember every word Jesus spoke that night. They wanted to remember Jesus' love for them.

Peter lies about knowing Jesus.

Matthew 26:69-75; Mark 14:66-72;
Luke 22:55-62; John 18:15-18,25-27

Peter lies about knowing Jesus.

Matthew 26:69-75; Mark 14:66-72; Luke 22:55-62; John 18:15-18,25-27

Jesus had been arrested by people who wanted to hurt Him. Peter was scared. He was afraid he might be arrested, too. A servant girl asked Peter if he was one of Jesus' friends. Peter lied. "I don't know what you are talking about," he said. The servant girl told some other people that she thought Peter was one of Jesus' friends. Peter got angry and said, "I don't know Him!"

Later on some other people said, "You must be one of Jesus' friends." Peter was still afraid and said, "I don't know the man!" Right away a rooster began to crow.

Suddenly Peter remembered Jesus' words. Jesus had said that Peter would lie about Him three times before a rooster crowed in the morning. Peter didn't want to lie about Jesus because Peter loved Jesus very much. Peter was very sorry that he had lied about Jesus. Peter went outside and cried. Later, Jesus showed that He still loved Peter, and He forgave Peter.

Jesus dies on the cross.
Matthew 27:32-56; Mark 15:21-41;
Luke 23:26-49; John 19:17-37

Jesus dies on the cross.

Matthew 27:32-56; Mark 15:21-41; Luke 23:26-49; John 19:17-37

One day, Jesus told His friends, "In a few days, some people are going to take Me away. I'm going to be killed." Jesus' friends were sad. Jesus knew this was part of God's plan so people could be forgiven for wrong things they have done. And Jesus knew He wouldn't stay dead!

The people who wanted to kill Jesus did not like it that so many people loved Him. When these people came to get Jesus, Jesus let them take Him. And He let them kill Him on a cross.

Jesus' friends were sad. They took Jesus' body and put it into a tomb. A tomb was a little room cut out of the side of a hill. Some men put a huge rock in front of the doorway of the tomb. Jesus' friends were very sad. They didn't know that something wonderful was going to happen.

Jesus rises from the dead.
Matthew 28:1-10

Jesus rises from the dead.

Matthew 28:1-10

When Jesus was here on Earth, He did many wonderful things. He made blind people see. He made crippled people walk again. He taught people about God. Jesus loved people very much. But not everyone loved Jesus.

Some of the leaders hated Jesus. In fact, they wanted to get rid of Jesus. They didn't like it that so many people wanted Jesus to be their leader! These people decided to kill Jesus. Jesus knew that the reason He came to Earth was to take the punishment for all the wrong things people had ever done or ever would do. Jesus knew God was in charge of what was happening. So Jesus let the angry leaders kill Him on a cross.

Jesus' friends were very sad. They put Jesus' body in a tomb in a garden and rolled a big rock in front of the doorway.

On the first day of the week, two of Jesus' friends walked to the garden where the tomb was. These women were sad that their wonderful friend Jesus was dead. But when the women got to the tomb, the huge rock in front of the doorway had been moved. They looked inside. Jesus' body was gone!

Suddenly, the women saw two angels. "Why are you looking for Jesus here?" the angels asked. "Jesus is not dead. He is alive! He is risen—just as He told you."

The women were glad! They ran to tell others the good news. As they ran, Jesus met them. Jesus said, "Don't be afraid." Then the women told Jesus' friends that Jesus is alive!

Jesus talks to Mary
in the garden.
John 20:10-18

Jesus talks to Mary in the garden.

John 20:10-18

Mary felt very sad. She thought she would never see Jesus again. Mary went to the tomb where Jesus' body was. Mary wanted to put some spices on Jesus' body (as people did in Bible times when someone died).

When Mary got to the tomb, she saw that it was empty! Jesus' body wasn't there anymore. Mary cried and cried. She didn't know that Jesus was alive. Mary saw two angels. They asked, "Why are you crying?"

Mary said, "Someone has taken Jesus' body and I don't know where they have put it." Then Mary turned around and saw a man standing there.

"Woman," the man said, "why are you crying? Who are you looking for?" Mary thought that He was a gardener.

Mary said, "Sir, if you have taken him away, tell me where you have put him."

The man just said her name, "Mary." Right away Mary knew that He was Jesus and He was alive! Mary felt so happy! Jesus told Mary to go and tell His friends that He was alive.

Two friends see Jesus.
Luke 24:13-35

Two friends see Jesus.

Luke 24:13-35

Two of Jesus' friends were on their way to a little town named Emmaus. They were very sad because Jesus had died. As the two friends walked, a man began to walk with them. He asked them what they were talking about.

"We are talking about Jesus," they answered. "Haven't you heard about all that's happened in Jerusalem? Jesus was killed on a cross. That was three days ago. But now some women have told us that Jesus is not dead. They say He is living!"

The man walked quietly beside the two friends. He listened to everything they told Him. Then He told them some wonderful things. "Long ago," He said, "God promised to send a Savior into the world. God said that this Savior would die and that He would live again."

When they reached the town of Emmaus, it was getting dark. The friends invited the man to stay and eat with them. Before they ate, the man thanked God for the food. Then He tore the bread and gave them pieces of it. Suddenly, the two friends knew this man was JESUS! But then, Jesus was gone! The friends were amazed—they had seen that Jesus is alive!

The two friends were so excited, they ran all the way back to Jerusalem! They ran to Jesus' other friends. "It's true!" they said. "Jesus IS alive! We walked with Him. He told us wonderful things!" The friends told what Jesus had said. And everyone was happy that Jesus is alive!

Jesus talks to His friends.

Mark 16:14; Luke 24:36-43; John 20:19-23

Jesus talks to His friends.

Mark 16:14; Luke 24:36-43; John 20:19-23

Most of Jesus' special friends were together in a room with the doors locked. They were afraid that the people who killed Jesus would try to hurt them, too.

Suddenly Jesus was in the room with them! He didn't come through the door—it was locked. He didn't come through the windows—they were shut. He just appeared!

Jesus said, "Peace be with you." His friends were afraid! They thought Jesus was a ghost. "Why are you afraid?" Jesus asked. "Why don't you believe that it is really me? Touch me and see that I am really alive. I'm not a ghost." Jesus showed them His hands and His feet that still had marks from when He was on the cross. Jesus even ate some fish with them. Jesus explained to them that He had to die on the cross so that people everywhere could have their sins forgiven. Finally, the friends believed that Jesus really was alive. They were so happy!

Thomas believes when he sees Jesus.

John 20:24-29

Thomas believes when he sees Jesus.

John 20:24-29

Some of Jesus' friends were excited! "We have seen Jesus!" Jesus' friends said. "He is alive!"

Thomas was sad. Thomas knew that Jesus had died. Thomas didn't believe that Jesus had come back to life. "I won't believe that Jesus is alive unless I see Him and touch Him," Thomas said.

Later Thomas and Jesus' other friends were together in a house. The doors were locked so that no one could get in. Suddenly, Jesus appeared in the room. Jesus knew that Thomas still didn't believe He was really alive. Jesus must have smiled at Thomas. "Come and touch Me, Thomas," Jesus said. "I want you to know that I am alive." Thomas was glad to see Jesus! Now Thomas knew for sure that Jesus was alive.

Jesus cooks breakfast
on the beach.
John 21:1-25

Jesus cooks breakfast on the beach.

John 21:1-25

After Jesus died and came back to life, some of Jesus' friends went fishing. They fished all night long, but didn't catch any fish. They were still in their boats on the lake when morning came. As it got light, they could see someone standing on the beach. He called out, "Do you have any fish?"

Jesus' friends answered, "No."

"Throw your net on the right side of the boat and you will find some fish," the man said. When Jesus' friends threw out the net, they caught so many fish that they couldn't pull the net back onto the boat. Peter knew it was Jesus talking to them! Peter jumped into the water and swam to the beach to see Jesus. The others followed in the boat. They towed the net full of fish behind them.

When they got to the shore, they saw that Jesus was cooking breakfast. There was a fire with some fish on it and some bread. Jesus invited them to have breakfast with Him.

Jesus makes a promise.
Matthew 28:16-20

Jesus makes a promise.

Matthew 28:16-20

After Jesus died and came back to life, He spent time with His friends. One time, Jesus appeared in a room where all His friends were gathered. Another time Jesus cooked breakfast for His friends on the beach. Jesus told His friends more about why He died and came back to life again. He also told them about God's good plans for them and the whole world.

One day Jesus talked to His friends while they were on a hillside near the Sea of Galilee. "I want all the people in the world to know about Me and My love for them," Jesus said. "And I want you to teach people everywhere to obey what I taught you about how to live. Baptize them and teach them how to be My followers." But Jesus' friends were just a few people. How could they tell all people in all the places in the world about Jesus?

Jesus didn't expect His friends to do this big job all by themselves! Jesus promised that He would be with His friends. Even though they wouldn't see Him, Jesus would always be with them. Jesus said He would send the Holy Spirit to give them power to tell the good news about Him. Jesus' friends were glad to hear Jesus' promise! They knew Jesus would keep His promise to them.

Jesus goes back to heaven.
Luke 24:50-53; Acts 1:1-11

Jesus goes back to heaven.

Luke 24:50-53; Acts 1:1-11

After Jesus came back to life, He spent many days talking to His friends. One day they went to the top of a hill. "Tell people all over the world about Me," Jesus said. Jesus promised that the Holy Spirit would come and make them able to do everything Jesus asked them to do.

Then Jesus went up to heaven. Jesus' friends watched as Jesus went up in the air. Soon Jesus was covered up by clouds. Jesus' friends couldn't see Him anymore, but they kept looking up for a while.

Suddenly two angels stood beside them. "Why do you stand here looking into the sky?" They asked. "Jesus will come back someday the same way you saw Him go up into heaven." Then Jesus' friends went to Jerusalem to pray and wait for the Holy Spirit to come.

God sends the Holy Spirit.

Acts 2:1-13

God sends the Holy Spirit.

Acts 2:1-13

After Jesus went back to heaven, His friends prayed and stayed together in Jerusalem. One morning, a sound like a strong wind blowing filled the house where they were staying. Something that looked like a small fire sat on top of each person's head! The Holy Spirit Jesus promised had finally come!

There were people from many different places staying in Jerusalem. These people spoke many different languages. When they heard the noise, they gathered around the house to see what was going on.

Jesus' friends began to speak in other languages, telling all the people about Jesus. The people in Jerusalem were amazed because they heard what Jesus' friends were saying about Jesus in their own languages! Many people believed in Jesus and started to tell other people about Jesus, too.

God's family meets together.
Acts 2:42-47; 4:32-35; 5:12-16

God's family meets together.

Acts 2:42-47; 4:32-35; 5:12-16

Jesus' followers were telling more and more people the good news about Jesus. And more and more people were becoming part of God's family.

This family of believers met together every day. They sang and praised God! They talked to each other about Jesus. They ate meals together. And they prayed together often.

The people in God's family loved being together. They showed that they loved each other by taking care of each other. They shared all the things they had. People sold things they owned so that they could have money to help others who needed food or clothes.

God helped Jesus' followers learn how to love each other and love the people around them. The people in God's family wanted everyone to know the good news about Jesus. The good news about Jesus spread throughout the city of Jerusalem. And every day, more and more people chose to become followers of Jesus!

Peter helps a lame man.
Acts 3:1-16

Peter helps a lame man.

Acts 3:1-16

Every day hundreds of people worshiped God in the Temple in Jerusalem. On their way to the Temple, these people walked through the Temple gate. One man sat by the gate, begging. This man was lame. His feet and legs didn't work. He couldn't walk or run. The lame man asked people who walked by him to put money into his bowl.

One day, Peter and John were on their way into the Temple. The lame man asked them for money. But Peter knew the lame man needed something else. Peter said, "I have no silver or gold to give you. But I will give you what I do have." Peter took the man by the hand. He helped him to his feet and said, "In the name of Jesus, walk!" And the man did!

Now the man could jump! Now the man could leap! He was so excited and happy, he went into the Temple with Peter and John. The lame man praised God! The people in the Temple were amazed. They were surprised that the lame man was now jumping and walking.

Peter said, "Why are you surprised? It is the power of God that has made this man completely well! And this same God sent Jesus to you." The people listened as Peter told them about God's Son, Jesus. Many people who heard believed in Jesus and became part of God's family!

Hungry widows are given food.
Acts 6:1-7

Hungry widows are given food.

Acts 6:1-7

Every day, Jesus' followers told others about Jesus. More and more people learned to love Jesus. And every day, people who loved Jesus shared their food and clothing with those who did not have enough.

Some of the people who didn't have enough food or clothes were widows. (A widow is a woman whose husband is dead.) These women needed help getting food. Some of their friends told the church leaders about the widows who needed food.

The church leaders listened carefully. They were sorry that these women did not have enough food.

"Choose seven helpers," the leaders said. "These helpers will make sure everyone gets enough food." So the people chose seven men. Then the leaders prayed for these men. They asked God to help them do their work fairly and kindly.

The helpers did a good job! They made sure everyone got the food they needed. Now the widows had enough food to eat. Being kind was one way Jesus' followers showed they loved Jesus.

Philip tells the good news about Jesus to an Ethiopian man.
Acts 8:26-40

Philip tells the good news about Jesus to an Ethiopian man.

Acts 8:26-40

An angel told Philip to walk on a certain road in the desert. Philip did what the angel said. As he walked, Philip saw a man riding in a chariot. This man worked for the queen of Ethiopia. He was reading a scroll with words from the Bible.

God told Philip to go to the man's chariot and stay with it. Philip had to run to catch up with the chariot. Philip heard the man reading words from the Bible. Philip asked the man if he understood what he was reading. The Ethiopian man said, "How can I unless someone explains it to me?" The man invited Philip to ride with him in the chariot.

Philip explained that the words the man was reading told about Jesus. Philip told the man that Jesus died and came back to life again so people who believe in Jesus can live forever with Him. When they came to some water, the man stopped the chariot. To show that he believed in Jesus, Philip baptized him. Then Philip disappeared! God took Philip to another place. The Ethiopian man went back home happy because he knew Jesus.

Jesus talks to Saul.
Acts 9:1-19

Jesus talks to Saul.

Acts 9:1-19

Saul was certain that Jesus' friends were telling lies. Saul didn't believe that Jesus was God's Son. Saul wanted to make people stop talking about Jesus. Saul was so angry that he even wanted to kill people who believed in Jesus!

Saul went to Damascus to find people who believed in Jesus and take them as prisoners to Jerusalem. As he walked along the road with some friends, a bright light suddenly flashed around Saul. Saul fell to the ground. Jesus talked to Saul. "Why are you hurting me?" Jesus said. "Go to Damascus and you will be told what you must do." Saul got up, but he could not see. Saul's friends helped Saul walk to Damascus.

For three days, Saul was blind and he didn't eat anything. He prayed to God. God sent a man who loved Jesus to help Saul. The man went to the house where Saul was staying and said, "The Lord Jesus sent me so that you may see again." Right away, Saul could see. Now Saul loved and obeyed Jesus.

Ananias obeys God.
Acts 9:10-22

Ananias obeys God.

Acts 9:10-22

A man named Ananias lived in Damascus. He was a follower of Jesus. Ananias loved God very much. One day, Ananias heard a message from God. God told him to go to a certain house to pray for a man named Saul.

But Ananias was afraid of Saul. Saul had tried to stop Jesus' followers from telling about Jesus. In fact, Saul had come to Damascus to put Jesus' followers into jail! God told Ananias that He had chosen Saul to tell many people the good news about Jesus!

So Ananias obeyed God. He went to the house where Saul was staying. "Jesus has sent me here so that you can see again," Ananias said.

Ananias put his hands on Saul and prayed for him. Something like scales fell from Saul's eyes. Saul could see again! Soon, Saul began telling others in Damascus about Jesus. Ananias and the other followers of Jesus were amazed and glad!

Saul escapes in a basket.

Acts 9:19-25

Saul escapes in a basket.

Acts 9:19-25

Saul was telling the good news about Jesus. Many people were surprised because Saul used to hate people who loved Jesus. Saul used to put people who worshiped Jesus in jail. But now Saul loved Jesus too, and he wanted other people to know about Jesus. Saul told many people that Jesus was really God's Son.

Some people were angry that Saul was preaching about Jesus. They made a plan to kill Saul. They waited by the gates to the city. They wanted to catch Saul going somewhere by himself. Then they could kill him!

Some of Saul's new friends found out about the plan to hurt Saul. In the middle of the night, Saul's friends put Saul in a big basket and lowered it down over the wall. Saul escaped from the people who wanted to kill him!

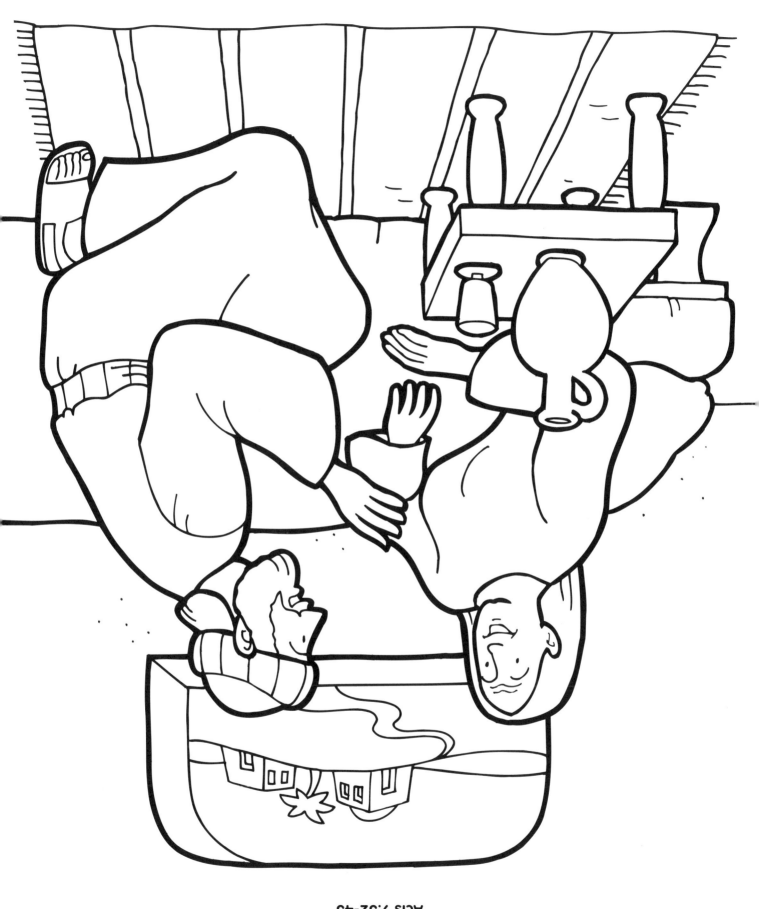

God brings Dorcas to life again after Peter prays.
Acts 9:32-43

God brings Dorcas to life again after Peter prays.

Acts 9:32-43

Dorcas loved to help other people. She made clothes for others. She always helped the poor. She always tried to do good things. All the people in her town really loved her.

But Dorcas got very sick, so sick that she died. Her friends were very sad. Some of Dorcas's friends heard that Peter, Jesus' friend, was in a nearby town. They went to see Peter, and asked him to come to see Dorcas.

Peter came. Dorcas's friends took him to the room where Dorcas was. Peter told them all to leave the room. Peter got down on his knees and prayed. Then Peter looked at Dorcas and said, "Dorcas, get up." She opened her eyes and sat up. Peter helped her up and led her downstairs to where her friends were waiting. She was alive! Many people in Dorcas's town believed in Jesus because God made Dorcas alive.

Peter learns about God's love for all people.
Acts 10:9-48

Peter learns about God's love for all people.

Acts 10:9-48

A man named Cornelius loved God. One day while Cornelius was praying, God sent an angel to him. The angel told Cornelius to send for a man named Peter. Peter lived in Joppa. Right away, Cornelius sent three helpers to Joppa to invite Peter to visit.

When the helpers came to Joppa, Peter was up on the flat roof of the house. He was praying. God showed Peter a strange dream. In the dream, a big sheet came down from the sky. In the sheet were frogs, lizards, pigs and horses.

God said to Peter, "Peter, you can eat any of these animals." But Peter knew that it was against God's rules to eat these kinds of meat. But God showed this dream to Peter two more times! Then Peter heard the helpers calling for him.

When Peter went downstairs, the three helpers were waiting at the gate. They were Gentiles. Jews were supposed to stay away from Gentiles. Then Peter understood the dream. All the people God created, both Jews and Gentiles, could be a part of God's family.

Peter went with the men to Cornelius's house. The house was full of people. They all wanted to hear about Jesus. Peter said to them, "I now know that God loves every person. He has sent me to tell you the good news about Jesus." The people believed what Peter told them. They became a part of God's family!

An angel frees Peter.

Acts 12:1-19

An angel frees Peter.

Acts 12:1-19

King Herod put Peter in prison. He decided to kill Peter because some angry men did not want Peter to keep preaching about Jesus. That night Peter slept chained to two guards in his prison cell. More guards stood at the entrance. They didn't want Peter to escape!

Suddenly an angel appeared in Peter's prison cell. The angel said, "Quick, get up!" The chains fell right off Peter's wrists. Then the angel told Peter to get dressed and follow him. They walked out of the prison, right past the guards. The gate to the city even opened by itself to let them in! Then the angel disappeared!

Peter quickly went to a house where some other believers in Jesus were praying for him. Peter knocked on the door. The servant girl who came to the door was so surprised that she forgot to open the door and let him in! When Peter finally was let into the house, he explained to everyone what had happened. They all praised God together for answering their prayers and rescuing Peter.

Timothy learns about God and shares the good news.
Acts 16:1-5; Philippians 2:19-22; 1 Thessalonians 3:2-10; 2 Timothy 1

Timothy learns about God and shares the good news.

Acts 16:1-5; Philippians 2:19-22; 1 Thessalonians 3:2-10; 2 Timothy 1

Timothy was a young man. Timothy's grandmother Eunice and his mother, Lois, believed in God. As Timothy grew up, they told him stories about God's love and faithfulness. Timothy believed God's Word and wanted to love and obey God.

While Timothy was still a teenager, he met Paul. Paul took Timothy with him as he traveled from city to city. Paul helped Timothy learn to share the good news of Jesus. Paul prayed for Timothy.

Later, Paul sent Timothy to take messages to other believers. Timothy cared for the people in these churches. He helped them learn about Jesus.

After Timothy had visited a church, he came back and told Paul how the believers there were doing. Timothy was a great helper to Paul.

When Paul was in prison several years later, he wrote Timothy letters. Paul told Timothy to love God and share God's love with others. Timothy's mother and grandmother and Paul taught Timothy. And many more people learned about Jesus and believed in Him because Timothy taught them!

Lydia believes in Jesus.
Acts 16:11-15

Lydia believes in Jesus.

Acts 16:11-15

Paul (who used to be called Saul) and some others traveled to another city. They looked for people who loved God and wanted to learn more about Him. Some women were sitting by the river. The women gathered there to pray and talk about God. Paul and the others sat down with the women to talk to them about Jesus.

"Jesus is God's Son," they said. "He died and came back to life again so that you can live forever with Him." Lydia heard what Paul and the others said. Lydia believed what they said. Lydia loved God. Her whole family believed in Jesus when they heard about Him.

"Come and stay at my house," Lydia said. Paul and the other believers stayed with Lydia for a while.

Paul and Silas sing praise to God in jail.

Acts 16:16-40

Paul and Silas sing praise to God in jail.

Acts 16:16-40

Paul and his friend Silas were put in jail because some people were angry with them. The jailer put chains on their feet. Paul and Silas didn't act afraid.

Paul and Silas sang songs and prayed to God. The other prisoners in the jail listened to Paul and Silas.

In the middle of the night, the ground began to shake and the walls of the jail began to crumble. There was a terrible earthquake and all the doors of the jail came open. The chains on Paul and Silas came off!

The jailer thought that all the prisoners had escaped. The jailer decided that it would be better to kill himself than to be punished for losing the prisoners.

Paul cried out, "Don't hurt yourself! We are all still here!" The jailer took Paul and Silas out of the jail and took them home to take care of them. Now the jailer wanted to know about Jesus. Everyone in the jailer's family heard the good news about Jesus and believed in Him.

Paul tells about God in Athens.

Acts 17:16-34

Paul tells about God in Athens.

Acts 17:16-34

One day Paul went to the city of Athens. Athens was a big city! The people in Athens didn't know about the one true God. They didn't know about God's Son, Jesus. They worshiped false gods.

Paul told the people in Athens the good news about Jesus. "I can see you are very religious," Paul said. "But you don't know the one true God."

"This God made the world and everything in it. He made the trees, the mountains, the rocks and the sky. He made all of us!" Paul said that this one true God wanted the people to stop sinning and

do right. God made a way for the people to do this: He sent Jesus. Jesus died to take the punishment for their sins. Then God raised Him from the dead.

Some of the people who heard Paul's words were glad to learn about Jesus. Soon these people believed the good news about Jesus! They became a part of God's family!

Paul preaches to an angry crowd.
Acts 21:17—22:21

Paul preaches to an angry crowd.

Acts 21:17—22:21

Everywhere Paul went he told people about Jesus. Some people were angry because Paul told about Jesus. These angry people saw Paul in the Temple in Jerusalem. "Look!" they shouted to the crowd. "This is the man we don't like!"

Soon everyone was shouting. Some men grabbed Paul and dragged him out of the Temple. Soldiers heard the noise and ran to see what was happening. The leader of the soldiers thought Paul had done something wrong. He put chains on Paul. Then he asked, "Who is this man? What did he do?"

Everyone started shouting at the same time! The soldiers couldn't understand what the people were saying. They took Paul away from the crowd. But the noisy crowd followed Paul and the soldiers.

Paul asked, "May I talk to the people?" The leader told Paul he could talk. When the crowd became quiet, Paul said, "I used to hurt people who loved Jesus. But now I don't. Now I love Jesus, too. God has told me to tell all people the good news that Jesus is God's Son. And I am obeying God."

A plot against Paul is discovered.

Acts 23:12-35

A plot against Paul is discovered.

Acts 23:12-35

Paul traveled everywhere, telling many people the good news about Jesus. When he was in Jerusalem, some of the religious leaders who did not love Jesus heard Paul talking about Jesus. They got very angry and had Paul put in jail.

Forty of the men who did not love Jesus promised each other that they wouldn't eat any food or even drink any water until they had killed Paul. Paul's nephew heard about the plan to kill Paul. He went straight to visit his uncle Paul in jail. He told him what he had heard. Paul called one of the guards. "Take this young man to the commander," Paul said. "He has something to tell him."

Paul's nephew went to the commander. "The angry men want to hurt Paul," the nephew said. "Forty men plan to kill him!"

The commander wanted to keep Paul safe. So he called for 200 soldiers, 70 men on horses and 200 men with spears. During the night, all 470 men and their horses started walking out of the city. What a parade! Somewhere in the middle of all those soldiers was Paul! The 40 men waiting to hurt Paul never saw him! Paul had escaped! Now he could keep telling people about Jesus!

Paul tells a king about Jesus.

Acts 25:13—26:32

Paul tells a king about Jesus.

Acts 25:13—26:32

One day soldiers brought Paul to a big city. Paul was put in jail there because some people did not want Paul to talk about Jesus. These people asked the governor to keep Paul in jail. The governor's name was Festus.

While Paul was in jail, a king and his wife came to visit Festus. Festus told them about Paul. "Let me hear this man Paul," the king said to Festus.

"All right," Festus said. "I will have Paul come from jail tomorrow so you can hear him talk."

The very next day, the soldiers brought Paul from the jail. Paul was glad he could tell the good news about Jesus. "Jesus is God's Son," Paul said. Paul told them many other things about Jesus, too.

Festus didn't understand what Paul was saying. "Paul, you're crazy," Festus shouted.

Paul answered, "I am not crazy. What I am saying is true. I pray that you will believe Jesus is God's Son, just as I do."

Paul's ship wrecks in a storm.
Acts 27:1-44

Paul's ship wrecks in a storm.

Acts 27:1-44

Paul and many other people climbed onto a big ship. Paul knew it would not be safe to travel on the sea at this time. He told the people on the ship, "If we sail now, we'll have problems." The people didn't listen. The wind began to blow. It blew the ship out to sea.

Then the wind began to blow harder and harder. Splash! Splash! The waves splashed high in the air and into the ship. The waves almost knocked the ship over! Big dark clouds covered the sky. Rain came pouring down. Everyone on the ship was afraid.

Paul had good news for the people. "Don't be afraid," Paul said. "No one will be hurt. God sent an angel to tell me that God will take care of all of us."

Early in the morning, the people saw land! They tried to sail to the shore. But the big, strong waves pushed the ship into some sand just under the water. Crash! The ship broke apart into little pieces. All the people jumped into the water. They found their way to the land. No one had been hurt. God took care of all the people.

A snake bites Paul.
Acts 28:1-6

A snake bites Paul.

Acts 28:1-6

Paul and all the people on the ship were safe after their ship broke apart. They swam or floated on pieces of their ship to an island called Malta.

The people who lived on the island built a fire and helped take care of all the people from the ship. Paul helped to build the fire, too. Paul picked up some wood to put on the fire. When he put the wood on the fire, a snake came out of the wood and bit Paul on the hand.

The people on the island knew this snake was dangerous. They thought that the snake's bite would make Paul die. But God didn't let Paul die. The snake bite didn't hurt Paul. The people on the island were amazed.

The believers in Corinth help others.
2 Corinthians 8—9

The believers in Corinth help others.

2 Corinthians 8—9

Many of Jesus' followers lived in Jerusalem. But some of them were very poor. They needed money to buy food and clothes. So Paul wrote a letter to Jesus' followers in the city of Corinth. "Save some money every week for the Christians in Jerusalem," Paul wrote. "They need your help."

The Christians in Corinth could have said, "Why should we help those people? They live so far away. God can take care of them!" But they didn't. Each week they collected money to send to Jerusalem.

Later, Paul sent another letter to Corinth: "I'm coming to get the money you have. I'll take it with me to Jerusalem." And that's just what Paul did!

The people in Corinth were glad they could give their money to help others. And the people in Jerusalem were thankful the people in Corinth had cared for them.

Live by the fruit of the Spirit.
Galatians 1:1-2; 5:16,22-23

Live by the fruit of the Spirit.

Galatians 1:1-2; 5:16,22-23

Paul wrote many letters to Jesus' followers. One group of people he wrote to were the Galatians.

Paul told the Galatians that God gives His Holy Spirit to help each member of God's family talk and act in good ways. Paul compared the way God's Spirit helps us grow to the way that fruit grows. He wrote about nine good things that we can grow in our lives when God's Holy Spirit is in us.

Love, joy, peace, patience, kindness, goodness, faithfulness, gentleness and self-control are all fruit of the Spirit. God's Spirit wants to help everyone in God's family grow this good fruit in their lives.

Paul writes letters to help others follow Jesus.
2 Timothy 1:1—4:22

Paul writes letters to help others follow Jesus.

2 Timothy 1:1—4:22

Paul wrote many letters to different churches and to different people. Paul wanted to tell others about Jesus. He wanted to help people who loved Jesus know the right things to do. Sometimes Paul wrote letters while he was on a trip. Sometimes he even wrote letters when he was in prison!

Paul wasn't put in prison because he did anything wrong. Paul was put in prison several times because some people didn't want him to tell other people about Jesus.

One time Paul was in a deep, dark dungeon. He wrote a letter to Timothy. Timothy was Paul's friend. Paul wanted to tell Timothy many things. Paul also wanted Timothy to come and visit him in prison. Paul helped Timothy learn how to live as a follower of Jesus.

Be careful to say good words.
James 3:2-12

Be careful to say good words.

James 3:2-12

James was one of Jesus' followers. He wrote a letter to some of God's family. We can read his letter in the Bible. One important thing James wrote about was how our words should show our love for God and others.

James said a person's words are like the bit in a horse's mouth. The direction the horse moves is controlled by the way the bit is moved. James also wrote about the rudder of a boat. The rudder is a part of the boat that can be moved to change the direction of the boat. The bit and rudder are both small, but they make big changes in how the horse or boat move! Our words are a small part of what our bodies can do, but the things we say make a big difference.

James also wrote that our words are like a small flame. It can catch a whole forest on fire! Just a few little words can cause a lot of trouble, too. Sometimes just a few words can lead to anger, murder or even war. Our words can do good or bad things, so we have to be careful about what we say.

James wrote to help us see how important it is to ask for God's help to say only good words.

John writes good news.

Revelation 1:1,2,9-11; 21:3-5

John writes good news.

Revelation 1:1,2,9-11; 21:3-5

When Jesus lived on earth, John was one of Jesus' best friends. One day Jesus went back to live with God in heaven. Then John told many people the good news that Jesus loves all people. But some people did not love Jesus. They did not like John, either. They took John away from his home and made him live on a lonely island.

John had to stay on the island a long, long time. Every day he thought about Jesus and prayed. One day when John was praying, something very special happened. John heard a voice say, "Write a book about the things you see. Then send the book to the people who love Me." John knew it was Jesus speaking to him!

Then Jesus showed John what heaven is like. He also showed John some things that will happen later. Jesus is going to come back! People who love Jesus will live with Him forever.

For many, many days John carefully wrote Jesus' words on special books called scrolls. In our Bible we can read the words about heaven that Jesus told John to write.

Jesus will return as King.
Matthew 27:11—28; John 18:28—19:16; Revelation 4—5

Jesus will return as King.

Matthew 27:11—28; John 18:28—19:16; Revelation 4—5

Long ago, the people in Jerusalem wanted a strong, powerful king who would get rid of the Roman rulers they hated. Many people wanted Jesus to be that king! So when Jesus had ridden a donkey into the city of Jerusalem, crowds of people welcomed Him as king.

But instead of Jesus becoming the king of the city, something very different happened. A few nights later, Jesus was praying in a garden. Soldiers arrested Him! They took Him to the Roman governor, Pontius Pilate. The religious leaders told Pilate that Jesus should be killed.

Pilate asked Jesus some questions. Even though he didn't find anything wrong with Jesus' words or actions, Pilate still agreed to have Jesus put to death on the cross. Pilate might have thought that was the end of Jesus, but it wasn't. Jesus came back to life after three days.

The Bible says that right now Jesus is in heaven. He is Ruler and King over all the earth. Some day Jesus will come back! Everyone will kneel down before Jesus and say that He is Lord. Jesus is the King of everything on the earth and in heaven. And because He died to take the punishment for our sins and rose again, we can be part of His family. He will come back as our King!

More Great Resources from Gospel Light

The Big Book of God's Amazing Animals
This book includes 52 lessons about a variety of animals that will intrigue kids, such as dolphins, penguins, koala bears, whales and condors. Each lesson relates facts about the featured animal to a particular Bible verse. As kids learn about fascinating animals that God created, they'll also learn about Him and how He wants them to live.
ISBN 08307.37146

The Big Book of Bible Skits
Tom Boal

104 seriously funny Bible-teaching skits. Each skit comes with Bible background, performance tips, prop suggestions, discussion questions and more. Ages 10 to adult. Reproducible.
ISBN 08307.19164

The Really Big Book of Kids' Sermons and Object Talks with CD-ROM
This reproducible resource for children's pastors is packed with 156 sermons (one a week for three years) that are organized by topics such as friendship, prayer, salvation and more. Each sermon includes an object talk using a household object, discussion questions, prayer and optional information for older children. Reproducible.
ISBN 08307.36573

The Big Book of Volunteer Appreciation Ideas
Joyce Tepfer

This reproducible book is packed with 100 great thank-you ideas for teachers, volunteers and helpers in any children's ministry program. An invaluable resource for showing your gratitude!
ISBN 08307.33094

The Big Book of Christian Growth
Discipling made easy! 306 discussion cards based on Bible passages, and 75 games and activities for preteens. Reproducible.
ISBN 08307.25865

The Big Book of Bible Skills
Active games that teach a variety of Bible skills (book order, major divisions of the Bible, location references, key themes). Ages 8 to 12. Reproducible.
ISBN 08307.23463

The Big Book of Bible Games
200 fun, active games to review Bible stories and verses and to apply Bible truths to everyday life. For ages 6 to 12. Reproducible.
ISBN 08307.18214

The Big Book of Bible Games #2
150 active games—balloon games, creative team relays, human bowling, and more—that combine physical activity with Bible learning. Games are arranged by Bible theme and include discussion questions. For grades 1 to 6. Reproducible.
ISBN 08307.30532

To order, visit your local Christian bookstore or www.gospellight.com

Gospel Light
God's Word for a Kid's World!

Honor Your
Sunday School Teachers

On Sunday School Teacher Appreciation Day
the Third Sunday in October

SUNDAY SCHOOL TEACHER APPRECIATION DAY
Third Sunday in October

Churches across America are invited to set aside the third Sunday in October as a day to honor Sunday School teachers for their dedication, hard work and life-changing impact on their students. That's why Gospel Light launched **Sunday School Teacher Appreciation Day** in 1993, with the goal of honoring the 15 million Sunday School teachers nationwide who dedicate themselves to teaching the Word of God to children, youth and adults.

Visit **www.mysundayschoolteacher.com** to learn great ways to honor your teachers on Sunday School Teacher Appreciation Day and throughout the year.

NOMINATE YOUR TEACHERS FOR SUNDAY SCHOOL TEACHER OF THE YEAR!
Winner Receives a Dream Vacation to Hawaii!

An integral part of Sunday School Teacher Appreciation Day is the national search for the **Sunday School Teacher of the Year.** This award was established in honor of Dr. Henrietta Mears— a famous Christian educator who influenced the lives of such well-known and respected Christian leaders as Dr. Billy Graham, Bill and Vonette Bright, Dr. Richard Halverson, and many more.

You can honor your Sunday School teachers by nominating them for this award.
If one of your teachers is selected, he or she will receive **a dream vacation for two to Hawaii,**
plus free curriculum, resources and more for your church!

Nominate your teachers online at **www.mysundayschoolteacher.com.**

Sponsored by

Gospel Light

*Helping you honor Sunday School teachers,
the unsung heroes of the faith.*

In Partnership With